GOD'S PROVIDENCE, MY PRIVILEGE

Miracles of the Winston-Salem Rescue Mission

A. NEAL WILCOX

8/23/2014

To my friend Ramona Lowman
may our good God bless
you and yours as you
seek to serve Him.

Prov. 3:5-6

Neal Wilcox

From the First President of the Mission Board

———————✦———————

I first met Neal Wilcox on a cold, wet Saturday in Greenville, South Carolina. He was conducting an auction in the War Memorial Chapel (on the campus of Bob Jones University) of items not reclaimed from the campus Lost and Found. I was at the auction because I desperately needed an umbrella. Because it seemed to rain every day in Greenville, at BJU, where we were both students in the 1950s, umbrellas were the most frequently lost items — and among the most plentiful.

The thing I most remember about Neal that day was his insistence on getting top dollar for every item auctioned, he even turned down the highest bid when he considered it to be too low. He was a stickler for frugality, a character trait that would serve him well all his life. I did purchase an umbrella that day, but left feeling I had overpaid. This began my acquaintance with Neal Wilcox, a relationship that has lasted for fifty-eight years.

Neal was born into a family of limited means and raised by his grandparents in eastern North Carolina. From this humble beginning, very few would have predicted the great success he would achieve in life. Neal seemed undaunted by the challenges he faced. To pay for his college education, he worked in the BJU Dining Common during the school year; and, during the summers, he went door to door selling Bibles, dictionaries and cook books. After graduation, he accepted a staff position at BJU.

In 1967, Neal became the first Executive Director of the Winston-Salem Rescue Mission, where for over thirty-three years he successfully led the Mission in such a way that it became a model for other rescue missions. Since I was privileged to help found the Mission and serve as the first president of the Mission Board, I saw firsthand the very difficult task Neal had been given in 1967 as well as the spiritual and social benefits that followed from his capable leadership. I've always understood that everything rises or falls on leadership. The success of the Mission is directly attributable to Neal's guidance.

As you read Neal's (and his wife Barbara's) story, you will come both to know and to be inspired by the account of how our Lord took an individual from humble beginnings and enabled him to do seemingly impossible things for God's glory. You will be truly blessed by this great man's book.

—Stuart Epperson

TABLE OF CONTENTS

DEDICATION

To my dear wife Barbara, with thanks to my Lord for the more than fifty years we have had together to serve Him. My special thanks for her help in writing this book, which chronicles our thirty-three years in the ministry of rescue and the life experiences God used to prepare us for that ministry. Your patient and willing heart to serve was a gift from God that I have been blessed to share.

To my wonderful daughter Beverly and her family, thank you for your continued support of the Winston-Salem Rescue Mission and dedicated service to our Lord in our church and our community. I am especially thankful to you and Dan for Ryan and Caroline, our two precious grandchildren. Along with your mother, your encouragement and support inspired me to write about God's miracles at the Winston-Salem Rescue Mission.

ACKNOWLEDGEMENTS

I owe thanks to so many people who have served alongside me, prayed with me, and encouraged me, not only in my ministry, but also in my endeavor to write this book. Foremost, I am deeply grateful for my wife and family who have been with me every step of the way. I cannot thank them enough for their patience and understanding.

I thank the Mission Board of Directors, especially those who served as president, whose direction, wisdom, and support helped to expand our ministry far beyond its humble beginnings in 1967. These servants of God faithfully served with me for the thirty-three years I was director of the Winston-Salem Rescue Mission.

Thank you to those who served on the staff and labored tirelessly with me to care for the Spiritual and physical needs of the men we served. Notably, I appreciate those who served more than twenty years: Mrs. Lois Bowman, twenty-two years; Rev. Bob McDaniel (deceased), twenty-eight years; and Rev. David Moxley, thirty-three years.

My thanks to the many churches and faithful pastors who supported the Mission with their prayers, finances, and being the missionaries who spoke in the chapel or brought a meal for the men.

I realized the providence of God at work when Rick and Donna Triplett became our neighbors. While living in southern Virginia, they saw a television news story about the Winston-Salem Rescue Mission. As a result, Donna took an immediate interest in my book and became the answer to prayer, which was a great encouragement that gave Barbara and me the confidence needed to start this book. We owe much to her for her dedicated editorial assistance throughout this project and will be eternally grateful for her help. In addition, I appreciate all those who have reviewed this work and provided their thoughtful insight.

I gratefully acknowledge with love and appreciation the needy that God sent to the Mission, as well as the support from the Piedmont area of North Carolina for their support in reaching the least, the last, and the lost with the love of our Savior.

I give my ultimate thanks to my Lord and Savior Jesus Christ for saving, calling, guiding, and sustaining my wife and me as we served the hurting at the Winston-Salem Rescue Mission. I pray this book brings honor and glory to Him.

FOREWORD

———————◆———————

A little boy sat comfortably on an exposed root of a
very large oak tree collecting acorns and placing
them in a neat pile in front of him. An older gentleman
interrupted his morning walk and stopped to chat with the
child. He asked, "Do you know that this big oak tree was
once a small acorn?" This was baffling to the lad. As soon
as his visitor left, the lad stood up, walked a few feet from
the tree and began to measure the acorn and the oak. It just
isn't possible, he thought. These same thoughts flood my
mind whenever I reflect on the first home for the Winston-
Salem Rescue Mission and compare it to their present facilities and ministry.

Impossible! Incredible! Unbelief has an arsenal of words
to challenge our faith. However, from that very first day in a
small rented building to this present hour God has revealed
His omnipotence. Unbelief may chant "Impossible," but
faith responds: "God is able." And, He invites us to: "Come
and see."

In God's good providence, I was blessed to be a member
of the core group that was responsible for setting up the
organizational structure of the Mission, planning the first
budget, and securing the first director. To be truthful about
the matter, we had nothing to offer the director and his wife
but an opportunity — an opportunity and the promises of

God. It still amazes me. Neal and Barbara Wilcox were able to see the oak tree that would develop from a small acorn. For them, the will of God was enough!

Now, after a long and fruitful history the Winston-Salem Rescue Mission is a landmark in the city. Frequently, people use the Mission as a point of reference in giving directions on how to reach a local business or office. Then too, there is the lighted sign of the cross that distinguishes the location of the Mission at night. But just getting to the Mission is not the ultimate goal. All of the ministries of the WSRM are designed to point people to Christ and to give sinners the direction to Heaven.

This remarkable ministry of the love of God is a story that must be told. We are blessed indeed that Rev. Neal Wilcox, our first Director, has put in the tears and sweat to make this a reality by writing this book. Neal and Barbara gave their lives to the will of God, and the will of God used them to evangelize and enrich thousands of lives — turning tears of sorrow into tears of joy. Then, there was that special touch. Their daughter Beverly grew up in the Mission. The presence of a little girl at play softened the institutional aspect of the place and brought the fragrance of spikenard to the hearts of hardened sinners. Doubtless, in their minds, clients substituted another word for Mission — the word Home. In their earthly journey, the Mission became Home to sons, husbands, and brothers. Above all, the greater burden of the Mission was not just to provide a warm bed on a cold night, but to point men to the assurance of a heavenly Home through the finished work of the Lord Jesus Christ.

— Billy S. Martin

FOREWORD

———————◆———————

I have known Neal Wilcox for more than thirty years but did not know his amazing story. This friendly Southern Christian gentleman is another trophy of God's grace, patience and love. What a story Neal has to tell. Poverty, broken home, and broken relationships have broken many young men and women. His grandparent's love and faith—and lots of God's grace and miracles—make this an amazing saga of how God works in "His mysterious ways."

Since I too had worked while going to college, lived with my family above a rescue mission, and lived through a riot with guns blazing in our mission yard, I felt a close relationship with Neal. I can relate to Neal and Barbara's "adventure with God." Neal's worldly wealth upon graduation from college was an older car, a twenty-dollar bill and a college diploma, but he had "learned to live by faith." That is the story!

This is not a book about buildings, structures, and organizations. This is the story of how God uses individuals no matter from where they start when they make themselves totally available. This is a story of "miracles" as Neal shares the "impossible," and the stories of how broken people who had given up on themselves were "changed." I could not read those wonderful stories without tears.

I served with Brother Wilcox in the leadership of the Rescue Mission Movement. We walked together, prayed together, shared together, and sometimes disagreed, but we never were disagreeable toward each other. God brought this "Southern boy" and this "Minnesota lad" together to work for His Kingdom. This book is about heart, and I'll let Neal sum it up:

> *I heard it said, "To operate a rescue mission you need a warm heart and a tough hide." I asked the Lord to fill me with a compassionate love for these men and promised I would treat every man as I would want my dad to be treated if he came to the Mission. I wanted to show them God's unconditional, all encompassing love.*

> — Rev. Stephen E. Burger
> Former President and
> Executive Director (Retired)
> Association of Gospel Rescue Missions
> Kansas City, Missouri

INTRODUCTION

———————❖———————

*Therefore, my beloved brethren, be ye steadfast,
unmovable, always abounding in the work of the
Lord, forasmuch as ye know that your labor is not
in vain in the Lord.* 1 Cor. 15:58

What began in the spring of 1966 as a discussion among five preachers traveling from Winston-Salem, North Carolina to Hammond, Indiana, culminated in the establishment of the Winston-Salem Rescue Mission. As they traveled through the mountains of Tennessee, these servants of the Lord discussed the need for a place in Winston-Salem where homeless people could find help. Realizing they all shared the same burden, they prayed together with such fervor they wept. At one point, in order to see the road ahead the driver, Rev. John D. Moxley, had to stop to clear the windshield of the moisture that had accumulated because of their fervent prayers. Upon returning to Winston-Salem, they began to meet at Paul Meyers Bar-B-Que where they prayed and sought God's will for the Mission. With the Lord's leading, they quickly established a board of directors and set about the task of finding a mission director.

In early 1967, my wife Barbara and I were happily serving the Lord at Bob Jones University in Greenville, South Carolina, when Rev. Moxley and Stuart Epperson, a business man who was the president of the newly created board of the Winston-Salem Rescue Mission, interviewed me and offered me the director's position. Because Barbara and I were serving in a ministry we loved, among people with whom we had become dear friends, it was only after much prayer and discernment that I accepted the opportunity. The Lord had given me a heart for the hurting souls who wandered the streets, ensnared by their addictions and needing to know the love of God. Through prayer, I understood that this opportunity was God's calling for my life.

While Barbara and I knew this was God's will for our lives, little did we know what was in store for us or how God would use our life experiences to equip us to be His hands in the ministry to the homeless of Winston-Salem. I quickly understood that the Winston-Salem Rescue Mission was often God's last stop sign before a soul went out into eternity to meet his Maker.

I wrote this book to share the miracles in the ministry of rescue and to encourage and inspire the saints with a prayer that the unsaved will come to trust our Lord and Savior Jesus Christ. If you do not know Christ as your Savior, it is my prayer that you would see how good our great God is and that He came to seek and save those who are lost.

1

Rooted in Love

---·---

God in His infinite wisdom does not provide us with a detailed itinerary for our life's journey, but through His Word, and our understanding of it, He provides all the directions we need to reach the goal He has set for us.

My journey began on February 23, 1937, when my mom gave birth to me in a hospital in Nash County, North Carolina. Since my father (whom I never knew) was absent, she took me home to her parents' tobacco farm near Kinston, North Carolina. My mother was the seventh child in a family of thirteen. My grandfather would say, "I have twelve girls and every one of them has a brother." He was often asked, "Do you mean you have twenty-four children?" To which he jokingly answered, "No! I only had to have one boy for all the girls to have a brother."

My grandparents inherited several farms from their parents. The house in which I spent most of my early years had no electricity and, while there was a well with a hand pump behind the house, the water was unusable. Our "running" water was the water from a neighbor's well that we carried to our house in buckets. Granddad was semi-retired, so he rented his seventy-five acres of farmland to sharecroppers, Roscoe and Evelyn Simmons. They became great friends

19

of the family, so much so that when my grandparents, neither of whom had a driver's license, bought a new 1939 Chevrolet, the Simmons often acted as their chauffeur.

Soon after bringing me home, Mom left me in the care of my grandparents and her three young sisters to get a job in Kinston, twelve miles away. There, she stayed with her sister Betty Moore. Since she didn't have her own transportation, other folks carried Mom back and forth when she came to see me. I loved my mom and liked having her close. When the time would come for her visit to end, and she had to return to Kinston, my heart ached for her.

One hot summer day, when I was three-years old, someone came to take Mom back to Kinston. As the car left the yard, I wanted desperately to go with my mom. I could not help myself! I took off running into the cloud of dust that trailed behind the departing car. Soon the car disappeared from view, and I was left alone, sobbing in the settling dust. With tears streaming down my face, I slowly turned and headed back up that dirt road to my grandparents' home. I tried to wipe the tears from my eyes with my dusty hands, but that just irritated them. My eyes stung from the dust, which only added to the pain of my broken heart.

Granddad was my father figure from the time I was old enough to know him. During nice weather, Granddad would hitch his mule John to the cart, and we would go to the country store. Granddad's dog Jimbo followed along to protect us. Sitting beside Granddad on that twelve-inch board that served as the cart seat, with Jimbo chasing away anything that came into the road, I felt safe and secure. When we arrived, Granddad would buy me a large chocolate ice cream cone for a nickel. We sat around the pot belly stove with the other farmers and discussed the latest local events. In the winter, we talked about the weather. In the summer, we talked about their crops. As a young boy, I had little to add to the conversation but a lot to learn from it.

As I grew, Granddad would tell me, "Son, go hook John up to the cart and we'll go to the store." That's how he taught me. He gave me plenty of hands-on opportunities. Even though he had never received formal training, Granddad was the local veterinarian. Most folks thought he was very good at treating animals; he was the best they had. Occasionally, he took me with him on a veterinary call. Little did I know that this experience was preparing me for work I'd be doing years later on the Rescue Mission's farm.

I often think of my Grandmother in her homemade bonnet and apron, walking across the yard with her hands behind her back. Her apron was a part of her, emblematic of the hard-working farm wife of the 1940s. She might gather eggs in it; she might carry wood for the cook stove or anything else she wanted to carry. She was the spiritual leader in the home. She taught me Bible stories as we sat around the fireplace. The neighbors knew that if they had a biblical question they could get the answers from "Mrs. Irene." Grandmother was the most significant person in my early life. From the very beginning, she was the spiritual light in my life who prayed that I would trust the Lord for my salvation and that I would be called to preach. I have often said, "She prayed for me as she manicured her fingernails on the old scrub board behind the barn as she washed my dirty diapers in rain water caught in a wooden barrel from the barn's tin roof."

I spent those first five years in the loving watch care of a wise grandmother who knew that a child would not prosper under too many disciplinarians. Although my three young aunts all helped with my care, Grandmother said, "It would not be good having all you girls spanking him." So, she appointed Aunt Kyle to do any spanking that might be needed. Aunt Kyle loved and cared for me as though I was her own son. On Saturdays, she took me to a drugstore in Kinston that served fountain drinks and ice cream. She'd order our special treat for the week — two banana splits that cost twenty-five cents each. We would sit at the little table and chairs set aside especially for children and eat our treats. Those Saturdays with Aunt Kyle made me feel special. Even at my young age, I knew how hard she worked for the fifty cents a day she earned on Granddad's farm, yet she'd spend a whole day's pay on a treat for us.

A few years later, Aunt Kyle left home to take a good job caring for the little boy of a very wealthy family in New York City. When I got older I told her, "That good job was your reward for taking such good care of me." When she married Albert Shipley, Aunt Kyle moved to Chesapeake, Virginia. God blessed them with their own son, Anthony. Years later, I was privileged to attend her ninetieth birthday party. The bond between us never failed. The last two years of her life I was faithful to telephone her, no matter where I was. Just like we did on those special Saturdays when I was a little boy, we spent that special time together.

After I became a minister, Aunt Kyle often told me she wanted me to officiate at her funeral and asked how much I charged. I told her, "Aunt Kyle, I don't charge for funeral services. But, if you care to give me a gift, that is your decision." On January 4, 2007, I was honored to officiate at her funeral. Following the service, many of her family and friends commented to me, "You surely knew her well." With the hundreds of conversations we had over those two years before she died, I surely did know her. Aunt Kyle was the last of the thirteen children to pass away. Of those thirteen children, I officiated or took part in the funerals of seven of them. In the providence of God, I think that their love and closeness helped to compensate for my not having a dad.

* * *

When I was five, Mom came home with my stepfather, Bob Shirley. They took me to live in Ligonier, Pennsylvania. Leaving my familiar surroundings and the family I knew and loved, and adjusting to life that included a step-brother and a step-sister — both of whom were teenagers — was traumatic for me. That winter the snow was more than two-feet deep. The icicles that hung from the gutters of the house were more than two-feet long and bigger around than my stepfather's arm. I had never seen anything like that before. The next summer, my mother and us children crossed the creek behind our house to pick apples in the orchard about two hundred yards away. As we picked, someone shouted, "Is that smoke coming out of the upstairs window?" We dropped our apples and raced toward the house and found it engulfed in flames. No one dared to enter it to save anything. We had to relocate and start over.

One day I noticed Mom crying. Several weeks later, without explanation to me, she and I boarded a Greyhound bus back to North Carolina. We rode all night. As we arrived in Kinston the next morning, God painted the sky with a beautiful sunrise, as if to remind this little boy of the happiness he had known in this place. We rode the bus east on Highway 58 until the driver stopped to let us off at the same dirt road where, not so long ago, I had chased after the car taking my mom away. Mom carried a suitcase and I had a paper bag with a few clothes in it — the entirety of our worldly possessions. Mom was very quiet as we headed down that familiar dusty road to the home place, walking straight into the welcoming arms of the family we had left behind.

While we lived in Pennsylvania, the aunts I knew and loved moved to the city to find work, leaving my grandparents alone. I was told the family was not pleased when

Mom took me away. My grandparents would sit by the fireplace listening to their console radio, and whenever "Put My Little Shoes Away," a popular song of that day was playing, they had to wipe away tears because it reminded them of me.

* * *

After our return to the family, Mom stayed home for a few years. She got her driver's license, helped her parents, and took care of me. During these years, I grew even closer to my grandparents and learned many valuable lessons from them. There wasn't anything I wouldn't do for my grandparents. We had a special bond that the Lord graciously made possible for me in the absence of my dad. As a result, I have always had a great respect for and a desire to help the elderly. Years later, after I started the Rescue Mission, we provided "Senior Foster Care Division," a section reserved for senior citizens and disabled persons. Now, even after retirement, I enjoy conducting a weekly service at Shepherd's Care assisted living facility in Greenville, South Carolina. I am privileged to minister to some of the retired faculty and staff of Bob Jones University, who mentored me when I was a student.

By this time, most of my aunts were married and had families. Since they lived in the area, they would often visit their parents, bringing my cousins with them. I spent many enjoyable hours playing with my cousins. However, when they weren't around I spent many hours alone. I was often told by a family member, "If you don't find something to do, I will find something for you to do." At a very young age I understood I probably wouldn't like what they found for me to do, so I used my imagination and became very creative. I created an imaginary friend, Tommy Tinker. I liked Tommy because he never disagreed with me. Using materials available to a young farm boy in those times, I made my own darts by putting a nail in one end of a corncob and three tail feathers from Grandmother's rooster in the other end. I made my own bows and arrows. I even made my own baseball bats, face mask, and catcher's mitt. Since I loved to feed Granddad's pigs, I created my own game using corncobs as pigs and sticks for their pen. Tommy Tinker and I loaded my "pigs" in my toy truck and took them to market. My creativity was one of God's gifts I used later in my life to grow the ministry of the Rescue Mission.

The fall after I turned six I began my formal education at Trenton Elementary School, which was twelve miles away from home. Mom decided I should have a proper haircut to start school, so she took me to my first barbershop. Until that time, either one of my aunts or my mother had cut my hair. It was quite a big day when I climbed up into that barber chair for my first real haircut. Mom asked the barber to collect my curly hair so she could make a pincushion in memory of the occasion. I still have that pincushion seventy years later.

My mother was a seamstress, so many of my clothes were handmade. During those times, the feed we bought for our animals came in bags made from material that many women used to make clothes or cut into strips to make blankets. I would watch my mother as she sewed, and I wanted to learn how to sew. One of my fondest memories of my mom is the day she gave me some scraps and said, "Sew these together and make yourself a quilt cover and I will quilt it for you." I did it and was very proud of my accomplishment.

In the summer of 1948, Mom and I once again left the family home and moved into a small apartment in Kinston so she could get a job. Moving meant I had to change schools. That fall, I rode my bicycle the two miles to Harvey Elementary School. Transferring to a city school was a real challenge. I had finished fourth grade at Trenton, but Harvey wanted me to go through fourth grade again. My mom disagreed. I think that one of the loneliest moments of my life was walking alone down a long corridor at Harvey, not knowing anyone, and not feeling the love, care, and security I had felt at my grandparents' home. Eventually, I did make some friends, one in particular. Since we were both small for our age, we agreed that if anyone tried to hurt either of us, the other one would step in to help defend him. I don't remember that our agreement was ever tested.

Because changing schools was a challenge, and reasons Mom never discussed, we moved back to my grandparents' farm in January 1949. I returned to Trenton Elementary where I finished the fifth grade and passed to the sixth. At some time during those years, Granddad had a cancer removed from his shoulder and had to go out of town to get treatment. Mr. Killingworth, a friend of the family who had to undergo the same treatment rode with Granddad. After the treatments had been completed, Mr. Killingworth offered to pay Granddad for the rides. Granddad refused to take payment, so Mr. Killingworth gave me a little pig.

Just as I had done with my "corncob pigs," I used my energy and imagination to build a pig pen and care for my real pig myself. In the fall of the year, after the crops were harvested, I let my pig go "free range," a common practice among the local farmers. Farmers often used various patterns of ear notching and cropping to identify their pigs and keep track of them. The pigs usually came home to eat at least once a day. But there came a time when my pig was missing for several weeks. Fortunately, I found her in a cornfield with plenty of food and fresh water from a nearby spring. What more could a growing hog want? She had gotten so heavy that the skin and fat drooping over her eyes caused her to be blind. As a result, she couldn't find her way home. Granddad and I decided to take her to auction at Hookers Stockyard in Kinston. Weighing 350 pounds, she was the heaviest nine-month-old hog they'd ever sold, as of that time. I received a check for seventy dollars, which I set aside and later used to help pay for my first year of college.

After I had sold my hog, my uncle gave me another pig. When she was old enough, Granddad helped me take her to a neighbor's farm for breeding. We soon had a litter of pigs. Since I had become pretty proficient at raising hogs, one day Granddad said, "Son, you furnish the meat, and I'll furnish the bread." I did this until Grandmother died, and Granddad was put in a rest home. We raised and butchered at least two hogs a year, which provided us with sausage, country ham, pork chops, and chitterlings (hog intestines). My grandparents particularly enjoyed chitterlings. This experience served me in my ministry many years later as we raised animals on the Mission farm to provide pork and beef for homeless men.

* * *

In 1950, Granddad had a debilitating stroke that left him barely able to get from his bed to his chair. With some help, he could get to the front porch swing where he spent most of his days. Grandmother's health was also failing. Mom became their full-time caregiver. As my grandparents' health worsened, family members would come in and care for them at night so Mom could get some rest.

On May 28, 1951, Grandmother called me to her bedside just before she left for the hospital. She asked me to promise her that I would meet her over yonder, referring to Heaven. What could any grandson say to his beloved grandmother under such conditions? I promised her I would, even though my heart knew I was not prepared to do so. A few days later, as she lay in her hospital bed, she called her daughters to her bedside and said to them, "I want to see my baby girl Ozela." (Ozela had died at the age of 4 months and 21 days.) Grandmother then asked those around her to sing her favorite hymn, "Jesus Savior Pilot Me" written by Edward Hopper. On June 3, 1951, Grandmother went to be with her Lord and her baby daughter. The prayers she offered up for me during her life have followed me throughout all my days.

* * *

My Heavenly Father taught me love and compassion in my beloved grandparents' home. While beyond my comprehension as a child, He clearly was training me at such an early age to do a work for Him. In retrospect, it is so inspiring and exciting to look back on those years and see, from the beginning, God's leading hand on my life.

2

TO LIVE FOR CHRIST

---◆---

For as long as she lived, and her health permitted, Grandmother attended Shady Grove Methodist Church. During the time she and my aunts cared for me, I went with them. I read my Bible daily. I read Revelation over and over, not because I understood it, but because I wanted to be blessed like it says in Revelation 1:3, "Blessed is he that readeth, and they that hear the words of this prophecy...." I read my Bible before going to bed; and, when I laid my head on my pillow, my tears would chase each other down my cheeks. For you see, I did not understand how a lost soul could pray for a clean heart and forgiveness of sin by having faith in Christ's finished work on Calvary. I did not know how to trust Christ as my personal Savior.

Aunt Nanny McDaniel's oldest son Ed came by one August Sunday to take me to the Evangelical Baptist Church in Kinston. He had no idea I was faithfully reading my Bible, and, for several months, I had been under conviction of my need to trust Christ for my salvation. Dr. Oliver B. Green from Greenville, South Carolina, preached that morning. I don't remember much of the message, or even the invitation song, but when the invitation was given, I was inexplicably compelled to go forward in response to the conviction of the Holy Spirit. I then accompanied someone to the prayer room where we opened the Bible and read John 3:16, "For God so loved the world, that he gave his only begotten Son, that whosoever believeth in him should not perish, but have everlasting life." We also read Romans 10:13, "For whosoever shall call upon the name of the Lord shall be saved." We then read 1 John 1:9, "If we confess our sins, he is faithful and just to forgive us our sins, and cleanse us from all unrighteousness." After reading these scriptures, I prayed the sinner's prayer, "God be merciful to me a sinner and save me for Christ's sake, amen."

That Sunday morning, August 25, 1951, my heart and my life changed forever. It was the day I put my faith and trust in my Savior, Jesus Christ. I accepted Him and, praise the Lord, He accepted me! My life was put under new management. I had a new purpose! I was at peace, now knowing that I would see my grandmother again; and, although I never knew my earthly father, I met my Heavenly Father for the first time that day. Unlike my earthly father, my Heavenly Father assured me, "…I will never leave thee, nor forsake thee…." (Heb. 13:5) "And, being confident in Him, … I will not fear what man shall do unto me." (Heb. 13:6)

I found a special place in a sagebrush field on Granddad's farm where I could spend time alone with the Lord. In that place, my Heavenly Father provided me the strength and guidance I needed for my new life in Christ. My Father and I have had a wonderful relationship for more than sixty-one years, and my most treasured moments are spent in communion with Him.

* * *

I can't say that Ed realized the profound impact his kind act of taking his fourteen-year-old cousin to church would have. I prayed that someday the Lord would allow me to thank Ed properly for what he had done for me. Years later I visited Ed at his home to thank him. Ed simply responded, "I just did what I should have done."

Cousin Ed passed away the year following my visit. I was privileged to officiate at his funeral and share with his family and friends the story of my salvation in which he had played such an integral part. I told them every soul who found salvation in Christ at the Winston-Salem Rescue Mission was saved because Ed took me to church that August Sunday. With certainty, I assured them Ed's reward was waiting for him in Heaven, because the Bible tells us in Ephesians 6:8, "Whatsoever good thing any man doeth, the same shall he receive of the Lord...."

* * *

In October 1951, after Granddad was moved into a rest home in Raleigh, North Carolina, Mom moved back to Kinston. I was sent to live with Uncle Lee and Aunt Nancy Wilcox so I could complete the ninth grade at Jones Central High School. Uncle Lee was Mom's only brother. He and Aunt Nancy had two sons, Frederick and Harry, and a daughter Kaye at home.

After finishing ninth grade, I moved to Kinston with Mom and attended the same church where I had accepted the Lord. This was a difficult time for me. Mom became interested in one of the boarders, a traveling man, who rented a room from us. Mom was a professing Christian, and he was un-churched. The relationship broke my heart. I couldn't believe Mom would get involved with an unsaved man. At the age of fifteen, I knew enough from my Bible studies to know this was not the choice God would want her to make. This was my first encounter with a problem that was more than I could handle. My burden for the situation became so great that one day I locked myself in the bathroom, determined to stay there and pray until I found peace. For more than an hour I agonized with the Lord, weeping and praying that my Heavenly Father would end the relationship before it went any further. Finally, spent of emotion, having poured out my anguish to God, I washed my face, straightened up, and turned it over to the Lord. That night, the man moved out, never to be heard from again—an answered prayer. In 1 John 5:14-15, the Bible tells us: 14 "And this is the confidence that we have in him, that, if we ask any thing according to his will, he heareth us: 15 And if we know that he hear us, whatsoever we ask, we know that we have the petitions that we desired of him." This first real victory through prayer early in my Christian life shaped my prayer life and strengthened my faith because I knew a God who told me, "Call unto me, and I will answer thee, and show thee great and mighty things, which thou knowest not." (Jer. 33:3)

After spending two months with Mom, I moved to Aunt Nanny's house to help with the tobacco harvest. Aunt Nanny's son, Cecil, who had served in the Navy, had come home to tend the family farm. She and Cecil attended the Evangelical Baptist Church in Kinston—the same church I attended with her son Ed the Sunday I gave my life to Christ. She was a Sunday School teacher, and Cecil sang in the choir. These two dear people became very important in my life. God had once again provided me with godly role models—a mother and big brother. Besides working for Cecil, I helped other farmers, and the summer passed quickly.

I spent the next three years with Aunt Nanny and Cecil. Cecil taught me how to drive a tractor, do minor mechanical work on cars, and helped me to get my driver's license. He also taught me more about raising hogs and how to milk cows. I never had rebellious or resentful feelings about anything they asked me to do. I often said, "If Cecil had asked me to climb a greased pole backwards, I would have put it in reverse and tried!" Everything I learned under Cecil's guidance was further preparation for the life that God had waiting for me in Winston-Salem.

I completed my public education at Southwood High School, which was less than a mile from Aunt Nanny's house. My first year at Southwood I played first string on the school's baseball team. I studied agriculture and industrial arts. More importantly, I had opportunities to witness for the Lord. I could only think that Grandmother's heart would have been gladdened to see how God was working in my life at this time. Once, I brought several fellow students to my church revival. God worked in their hearts, and soon a group of us gathered regularly in the school library for prayer services. By the time I was seventeen, the Lord had called me to preach, an answer to my grandmother's fervent prayer for me. I preached my first message at a cottage prayer meeting in a home in Kinston. When a teacher asked me to speak in chapel, I took a stand against worldliness that led to my being sent to the principal's office. I had spoken to make it clear what the Bible tells us about the world and our relationship with God, "And be not conformed to this world: but be ye transformed by the renewing of your mind, that ye may prove what *is* that good, and acceptable, and perfect, will of God." (Rom. 12:2) My senior year I led the Youth for Christ services at my church. One evening, a 104-year-old lady attended the youth service and accepted the invitation to trust Christ. I was blessed to learn through her family that salvation had changed her life.

In my junior year, Mom had told me I could quit school. I told her I'd come too far not to finish. The last semester of my senior year I learned I needed a Civics class before I could graduate. The course was not offered that semester. Through the providence of the Lord, one of my teachers offered to tutor me in his home, and I was given credit for the course. I wanted to pay my teacher, but he would not accept payment. Aunt Nanny suggested I should give him some pork chops, a product from the hogs I had raised. I did. Following my graduation in May 1955, I worked on Aunt Nanny's farm for one more summer.

* * *

Throughout my stay with Aunt Nanny, I was in church every time the doors opened. Cecil and I went to revivals, tent meetings, and cottage prayer meetings — anywhere the Word was preached. We hungered for the Word of God. I went forward at every altar call to reaffirm my commitment to Christ and pray, "Lord, take me; mold me; make me; break me, please use me." As I was coming home from church one evening, I met a prison trustee who had been let outside his jail cell to get some fresh air. Once again the Lord worked in my life. Through His grace, I led that man to the Lord that evening. This experience gave me a burden for the lost. My heart was filled with gratitude for how God was working through me, and I told him I wanted to serve him twenty-four hours a day. The Lord blessed my request to serve by providing me a ministry in rescue. When we opened the Rescue Mission to help lost souls we operated twenty-four hours a day, seven days a week.

Russell Ridgway, an evangelist, came to our church. He wanted me to accompany him to Whiteville, North Carolina, to attend a city-wide tent meeting. I knew the Lord would use me as He needed, so I went. I dusted chairs, set out song books, led the singing, and helped in the prayer room during the invitation. I was not on salary and had just about exhausted the few dollars I had with me. I prayed earnestly, knowing that the Lord is faithful to all who labor in His service and would provide my needs.

While in Whiteville, I visited the sick in the hospital. After praying with an elderly man, he chose to put a five dollar bill in my pocket as thanks. Once more, my gracious God had answered my prayers.

3

EARLY YEARS AT
BOB JONES UNIVERSITY

———————◦———————

B en Eaton, my friend of many years, attended my church
and graduated from the Baptist Children's Home at
the same time I graduated from high school. In the fall
of 1955, Ben left Kinston to attend Bob Jones University
(BJU) in Greenville, South Carolina. When Ben came home
for Christmas break, he asked me about my plans for the
future. I told him I'd probably just continue to help Cecil
on the farm. As the holiday season ended, Ben urged me to
go with him when he returned to BJU and encouraged me
to attend college. I told him I didn't have enough money
for college and that I'd have to work and save some. Ben
encouraged me to trust the Lord and go. Following many
prayerful hours, I remembered God's call to Abraham
when he was told to leave Ur, "By faith Abraham, when
he was called to go out into a place which he should after
receive for an inheritance, obeyed; and he went out, not
knowing whither he went." (Heb. 11:8) I understood that
I too was being called to "go out" not knowing what the
Lord had in store for me. In the assurance of God's Word,
I once more put my life in my Savior's hands.

I matriculated in the spring semester at BJU on January 25, 1956. I used my life's savings of three hundred dollars to help pay for that first semester. By working in the Dining Common, I earned a scholarship that paid another twenty dollars a month toward my education. My life at BJU was so busy that the first semester just seemed to fly by. While weekdays were devoted to study and my work, as a member of the preacher boys' class I went on extension every weekend. A couple of friends and I were fortunate to go to Travelers Rest, a small town north of Greenville, where we preached in a barbershop and handed out tracts at other businesses. As the end of the semester approached, I realized that I needed six hundred dollars to cover next year's education expenses at BJU. If I was going to return in the fall, I needed a job. I made my concerns a matter of prayer and trusted my Heavenly Father to guide my future. Unfailingly, He answered my prayers.

Clayton Hadley, an upperclassman, talked with me about a summer job with the Southwestern Publishing Company located in Nashville, Tennessee. The work involved selling Bibles, Bible study books, dictionaries, and the *Mary Liles Wilson New Cook Book*. To accept the job, I needed enough money to get to Nashville to attend the week of sales training, living expenses while there, and, at the end of my training, travel money to my assigned sales territory. It didn't occur to me that I had no sales experience. I had very limited cash, and statistics showed that most people who go into sales fail in their first month. However, one thing I did have was full confidence that my Heavenly Father would be there with me in this venture, so I didn't hesitate. By working extra hours in the Dinning Common, I managed to save enough money to pay my matriculation fee for the next semester, as well as an additional fifty dollars for the sales school and relocation expenses.

In the sales school, I learned I would have to work hard and master my sales pitch if I wanted to earn enough money to return to BJU that fall. When they told us we would be working ten-hours a day, six days a week, that didn't bother me in the least. Having been raised on a farm, long days and long weeks were a fact of life for me.

At the end of the training, I was assigned my territory, southeast Alabama, and my sales partner, an inexperienced young man from Greenville. We bought our bus tickets and headed off to Elba, Alabama. Our first week there we stayed in a boarding house. But, by the end of the week, we were blessed to find lodging in the home of Mr. and Mrs. Clark. Mr. Clark had joined the church under the ministry of Dr. Bob Jones, Sr. The Clarks were very pleased to have us stay with them for the summer. They became my very dear friends and bought several books from me.

My partner was not suited for sales work and soon returned home, leaving me to survive on my own. But I knew I was not alone because my Heavenly Father always assured me, "...Be strong and of a good courage; be not afraid, neither be thou dismayed: for the LORD thy God *is* with thee withersoever thou goest." (Josh. 1:9) I found a good church, and since I didn't have a car, one of the members picked me up for Sunday services. I enjoyed meeting people, so my job provided many opportunities for me to witness for the Lord.

During the training, we were told to use the down payments we received from our book orders to cover our living expenses while in our sales territory. I accounted for my expenditures by sending a weekly sales and expense report to my supervisor in Nashville, along with any extra down payment money I hadn't used for living expenses. I paid the Clarks ten dollars a week for my room and breakfast. Sometimes my customers were kind enough to share lunch with me, which saved some expense. I learned to live frugally, so much so that one week I lived on sixteen dollars. When my supervisor reviewed my expense report, he told me I needed to spend more money on food.

I didn't have transportation, so I walked door to door carrying my case of book samples in the withering heat of an Alabama summer. I faced menacing dogs and occasionally had to deal with an upset customer. Sometimes, as I walked home at the end of a particularly tiring day, I'd reflect on Colossians 3:23, "Whatsoever ye do, do *it* heartily, as to the Lord, and not unto men." and my spirit was immediately renewed, knowing that my work was ultimately to glorify my Lord. August was upon me before I knew it. I placed my book order mid-month and sent a card to my customers informing them of the date that I would be by to deliver their books and collect their final payment. I had been so successful in my sales that, when my book order arrived, Mr. Clark recognized that I needed transportation to deliver all my books, and he graciously offered me the use his old pickup truck.

Just before the date I was to deliver my customers' books, Mom called to tell me my beloved grandfather had passed away and the funeral was to take place in two days. Since I had committed the delivery date to my customers, I faced a difficult decision. Do I abandon my promised delivery date and attend the funeral? What would my witness be to my customers if I left? While my heart ached to be at my grandfather's funeral, I kept my word to my customers, remembering what the Bible says, "But whoso keepeth his word, in him verily is the love of God perfected: hereby know we that we are in him." (1 John 2:5) I made my deliveries and collected six hundred and fifty dollars from my customers, which I converted to traveler's checks. Payments in hand, I hitch-hiked back to Greenville. Reflecting on that summer, I saw that, through my sales experience, I had met a lot of people, made a lot of friends, and learned a lot about myself. I knew how much God had blessed me. He gave me the confidence that, with His help, I could sell books and make enough money in three months to last me for twelve months. He answered prayer and supplied my every need. I had earned the funds I needed for my next school year. Additionally, I would return to my job waiting tables in the Dining Common.

My second year at BJU challenged me academically. I had to study hard to make passing grades. In addition to my job in the Dining Common, I repaired umbrellas to earn extra money. Yet, I still found time to enjoy some of the many activities offered at BJU. With all my activities, I was quite busy and often had to remind myself of the reason I was in college. The year slipped by and, as the summer of 1957 approached, I looked forward to resuming my summer employment with Southwestern Publishing. I truly loved selling Bibles and bringing God's Word to the people I met.

I returned to Nashville for a refresher sales course and roomed in the Nashville Rescue Mission. The previous spring I'd met the son of Rev. Short, one of the directors at that mission. I was always seeking opportunities to preach, so on my first trip to Nashville I contacted Rev. Short. He gave me an opportunity to preach at the mission. Then, each summer when I returned to Nashville for refresher training, I stayed at the mission where I helped in the services.

My second summer working for Southwestern I was assigned to work with Ed Guerrant, a fellow BJU student. Our territory was Cleveland, Tennessee. A Christian couple, the Nortons, rented us a basement room and shared breakfast with us. The people in the area were very friendly. We attended a small Baptist church and enjoyed the fellowship of Sunday worship. Neither of us had a car, so we spent long hours wearing thin the soles of our shoes as we went door to door. Our hard work earned us enough money to fund our education at BJU for another year.

* * *

After graduation, Ed and I served the Lord in totally different locales. Ed and his wife Barbara spent forty years as missionaries in Papua, New Guinea. My wife Barbara and I spent forty years ministering to the lost in Winston-Salem (thirty-three years in the Rescue Mission and, following my retirement, seven more years supporting the work being done there). Yet, fifty years after that first meeting in 1957, Ed and I are once again worshiping our Lord together in the same church, Morningside Baptist Church in Greenville, South Carolina.

* * *

Upon returning for my third year at BJU, I was assigned to the bus boy crew in the Dining Common—a promotion that came with a whole different set of responsibilities. I did everything from greasing axels on the busing carts, to busing tables, to cracking eggs for the cooks to serve breakfast to the three thousand students who attended BJU. The mechanical skills I'd learned from Cecil came in handy the day I had to grease the axles of those twenty busing carts by myself. Mr. Davis, my supervisor, was not sure I'd get them all done, but I knew God would want me to persevere. As a result, I completed the work in three hours.

Following the spring semester of 1958, I returned to my job with Southwestern. That summer I was assigned to Travelers Rest, South Carolina, where I worked alone. At the beginning of that summer Mom bought me a 1953 Chevrolet, which made it much easier to cover my territory and deliver my orders. I stayed with Mr. and Mrs.

Mitch Batson, who remained my friends for years. I attended Second Baptist Church, where I made many lasting friends. The pastor, Rev. Jess Stephens, had a large family. Providentially, two of his sons and one of his grandsons worked at the Winston-Salem Rescue Mission many years later. In conjunction with my work scholarship, I earned enough money that summer to cover my next year's expenses at BJU. Some of my aunts also helped me. When I visited them at Christmas, they each gave me a five dollar bill. They seemed proud of my hard work, and I have always been grateful for their support.

That fall when I returned to campus and to my job in the Dining Common, Mr. Davis asked me to develop a new job—kitchen host. As kitchen host, I oversaw the work of the two hundred wait staff who worked in the Dining Common. Looking back, I see that experience as the Lord preparing me to make decisions for, and communicate with, diverse groups of people, a skill that served me well at the Rescue Mission.

4

BROKE, BUT BLESSED

———————❖———————

The summer of 1959 was upon me before I knew it. However, this summer turned out to be different. I did not return to Southwestern, but instead I took a job selling books for *Collier's Encyclopedia*. After completing sales school in Richmond, Virginia, I stayed at the home of Wade Powell in Roanoke Rapids, North Carolina. I had met Wade in a BJU prayer group, and we became friends. He had encouraged me to come with him to work for *Collier's*. Since we traveled around our sales territory in Wade's car, he received a small commission on my sales to help cover travel expenses. Wade's father, Sam Powell, owned and managed the Sealtest® milk distributorship in the area, so Wade and I delivered milk in the morning. In the evening, we still had enough time to visit homes to sell encyclopedias. Wade and I enjoyed working together, which made for a great summer experience.

We attended a fledgling church in a house in Gaston, North Carolina, a suburb of Roanoke Rapids. The pastor, Rev. J. C. Justice, was excited that we joined his congregation, and he even gave me the opportunity to preach. During the invitation one Sunday morning, a high-school girl named Barbara Jordan, whose parents belonged to the congregation, came forward and dedicated her life to the Lord. Toward the end of the summer, Barbara consented to one date with me. But, as we have since come to understand, the Lord had a greater plan for us.

When I returned to school that fall, I knew I could not complete my degree by the end of the year. Although I had paid all my education costs, I continued working in the Dining Common. Consequently, I had to take less than a full credit load of classes. Unsure of what I would do after graduation, and convinced that I would never pass classes in Greek and Hebrew, I changed my major in Bible to a major in Practical Christian Training. I believed it would be applicable and beneficial in whatever calling the Lord provided.

Wade and I returned to Roanoke Rapids and worked for *Collier's* during the summer of 1960. We had recruited eight young men from BJU to join us. They rented an apartment and, once again, I stayed in Wade's home. We returned to the church in Gaston, which had grown and moved into a new building. Over the summer, I developed a good relationship with Barbara's parents and, with their permission, began to date her regularly. Needless to say, I had become very fond of Barbara and her parents. Mr. and Mrs. Jordan did not have a telephone in their home, so when I returned to school that fall, Barbara and I communicated the old-fashioned way — we wrote letters to each other.

I was determined to complete my undergraduate degree and graduate in May 1961. After finishing the fall semester, I was blessed to receive a full scholarship for the spring 1961 semester. As graduation approached, I remember so well the notice I received from the school administration which stated, "You have absolutely completed all of the requirements for your Bachelor of Arts degree." College had been a wonderful time of growing and learning and building my relationship with God.

No one had ever told me I could borrow money to go to school, and it never crossed my mind to do so. I believed I was supposed to pay for my education year by year, so through hard work I did. By the grace of my Heavenly Father, I had reached my goal at Bob Jones University. When I graduated, I assessed my worldly wealth and realized that I owned an older car, I had a twenty-dollar bill in my pocket and a college diploma in my hand—never in my life had I felt so broke. But I did not owe anything to anyone except my Heavenly Father. I learned "living by faith" early in my life, and it sustains me to this day.

5

MY CALL TO MINISTRY

W hile I had accepted an offer to participate in a post-graduate special assistant position for the fall of 1961, I still needed summer employment. I met with a recruiter from Camp Reveal, a Christian camp for under-privileged youth sponsored by the Evansville Rescue Mission. Dr. Ernest I. Reveal, who had been the Mission director, was a man of prayer and held a strong faith that the Lord would provide. Before he passed away in 1959, Dr. Reveal had been a frequent speaker at chapel at BJU. I was excited about the opportunity to work in his ministry. I had always wanted to work with youth, and the prospect of earning twenty-five dollars a week, room and board, and the opportunity to go away to a summer camp and share the gospel was very appealing. Two weeks after gradua-tion I drove to Evansville, Indiana. I spent the next eight weeks working with campers who were juniors and seniors in high school, and I also preached at the Rescue Mission. Through this wonderful experience, the Lord continued to grow me into the person I needed to be to serve Him in the ministry of a Rescue Mission.

Barbara and I had corresponded all summer. After summer camp, I returned to Roanoke Rapids to see her.

She had graduated from high school that year and was looking forward to starting the one-year business program offered at BJU that fall. When the fall semester began, we both worked in the Dining Common, but maintained a professional relationship while on the job. Since I was on staff, we "dated" in the Dating Parlor.

As a graduate assistant I earned a small salary. Additionally, I could take twelve hours of coursework a semester. However, I still needed to supplement my income with other employment. During the two years of my assistant's contract, I also sold diamond jewelry for a company based in Mt. Vernon, New York. As you might guess, the first diamond I bought was for Barbara. We became engaged at Christmas 1961. During her high school years Barbara had worked at Rose's Department Store, so I often say, "I got a million dollar wife out of Rose's Five and Dime Store." God's plan for me blessed me greatly when He placed Barbara in my life. I could not have found a better "help meet" for the things that lay ahead in my mission work. Proverbs 18:22 tells us, "Whoso findeth a wife findeth a good thing, and obtaineth favour of the Lord."

We both worked and saved for our wedding. Barbara worked for the J.P. Stevens Company for a year before we were married. With family and friends in attendance and Mr. Fred Davis officiating, Barbara and I were married on June 2, 1963, in the church where we met, Roanoke Independent Baptist Church. We did not know what the future held, but we knew that, if we stayed close to Him who does, He would bring us through. When I accepted a full-time job in the Dining Common, Barbara returned to BJU and worked in an office there.

We continued to serve the Lord at BJU for the next four years. But I had a strong desire to find a ministry in which Barbara and I could serve together. I discussed this with Dr. Gilbert Stenholm, director of the ministerial class. Then in early 1967, Stuart Epperson and Rev. Moxley, members of the board of directors for the newly organized Rescue Mission in Winston-Salem, interviewed me for the director's position at the Mission. Through these men, our Heavenly Father revealed His will for our lives and set a new course for the remainder of our working days.

6

GOD'S RESCUE MISSION

———————•———————

Other mission directors advised us our Mission should be located in an area where the men who needed it could access our services. The Mission we were about to open on North Trade Street was surrounded by vines and brush that provided cover for the local alcoholics and occasional homeless outsiders who were passing through. This area was referred to by the police and those who hung out there as the "jungle." Abandoned cars sat across the street from the Mission. Often left unlocked, the homeless used them for overnight accommodations. Unfortunately, one man had fallen asleep while smoking. His cigarette fell on the seat, and he died from smoke inhalation. The open space beneath several old tobacco warehouses in the area provided these men shelter from winter's cold or summer's heat. This was where the Lord led Barbara and me to minister to hurting and homeless men for the next thirty-three years.

* * *

On June 1, 1967, Barbara and I moved into the apartment above the Rescue Mission, located at 824 and 826 North Trade

Street—the skid row district of Winston-Salem. Brother Don Cox and his wife Carolyn were dear friends of ours at BJU. Don had a pickup truck, and he took the day off from work to help us move. We loaded the truck and a rental trailer the night before so we could get on the road early the next morning. We arrived at the Mission by early afternoon of the following day. This was the first time Don had seen the building and the neighborhood in which we would live. When he returned home after helping us, he commented to Carolyn that he never hated to leave a friend as much as he did leaving us in that building on skid row in Winston-Salem.

As we opened the door to the upstairs apartment, we were surprised to find many of the local churches had painted our apartment and put new floor covering in the kitchen. When we moved in, I noticed that our apartment had no electrical outlet capable of supporting the power supply needed for an air-conditioner. I knew that life in the apartment without air conditioning would become very uncomfortable in the heat of a North Carolina summer. Charles Elliott, a dear brother from Cedar Forest Baptist Church, later installed the 220 volt line needed for the air-conditioner.

A few months before we arrived in Winston-Salem, a garbage truck had emptied the contents of a dumpster and compressed the garbage one last time before going to the land fill. When the truck arrived at the landfill the driver pushed the lever, and the refuse was pushed out. To his horror, a man's body tumbled out with the garbage. Apparently, the man had crawled into the dumpster, fallen asleep, and was crushed to death when the contents of the dumpster were compressed. The image of this accident was sealed in my mind and heart. For me, this tragic incident reinforced the need for a Gospel preaching rescue mission, a rescue mission that would feed the bodies and souls of homeless men in Winston-Salem, where the hopeless could find hope and redemption. The message of this story was always with me, reminding me of my vision for the Rescue Mission.

Our first board meeting took place soon after I arrived, and the board was ready to turn the Mission over to me. The building sorely needed to be renovated and brought up to code. Other than my skill in building pig pens, I had no construction experience and absolutely no knowledge of building codes. In answer to my prayers, Brother Moxley helped me plan the chapel layout to include two offices in the back, a platform in the front for the pulpit, a prayer room behind the pulpit, and a closet for storage. He understood the codes and knew what was needed to bring the building into compliance. He also determined the cost of the planned renovations. After talking with Brother Moxley, the Tuttle Lumber Company extended us a thirty-day credit plan to buy the material we needed.

With the help of some local church members and some college students from BJU who came with us to work in establishing the Mission, the renovations were soon underway. As we worked, some of the homeless men would stop by, which gave me an opportunity to get to know them before we opened the Mission. On July 1, we received our first bills. Veigh Meyers, our part-time secretary, and I checked our bank account. We found there was money to cover all the bills, but not enough for me to receive a full paycheck. I remembered what Rev. Wayman Pritchard, founder and director of the Raleigh Rescue Mission had told me, "God will always pay for what he orders, but you better be sure He ordered it." From that time forward, we always had sufficient funds to pay our bills on time and provide a full paycheck for me. Eventually, Barbara's training and experience made her an invaluable asset to the life of the Mission when she became the office manager. Prior to this she had worked at a local radio station, WKBX.

Gathering the supplies, furnishings, and the funding needed to establish the Mission and get it operational depended on community support. To that end, I visited churches every time there was an opportunity to share the vision God had placed on my heart. I preached in churches and spoke to civic clubs, men's groups, ladies groups, senior groups, teen groups, Christian schools, and even to a health club. When I was out seeking the support of other churches and groups, my Sunday School Class and my home church, Urban Street Baptist (later known as Vernon Forest Baptist), prayed for me and the ministry. It became self-evident that God touched the hearts of the people because soon churches were collecting clothing and furniture and bringing them to the Mission. We received a truck load of clothes from BJU. When BJU refurbished a dormitory that year, the Mission purchased some of their used bunk beds and mattresses for twenty dollars a set. Pilot trucking company delivered them to the Mission free of charge.

Our vision was spreading and God's people were responding. My Heavenly Father sent people who could fill the needs of the Mission.

- Billy Royal, an accountant who worked at the post office, volunteered to set up the accounting books and kept them for more than thirty-three years.
- Woody Lewellyn, a recovering alcoholic, owned a plumbing business and he volunteered to do the plumbing.

Billy Royal

- Rev. Stephen G. Tilley, a student at Piedmont Bible College (now Piedmont International University), helped us dig out and frame the steps from the rear basement to the main floor where the bathrooms were located. (He later became the Pastor of Parkland Baptist Church (now Parkland Church) and a board member for the Mission.) I called a cement company and asked them if they happened to have a truck with some extra cement after finishing a job, would they be kind enough to send it by the Mission to help me with the project. I told them we needed about a yard of cement. The company sent enough to complete the steps and make a ramp out from the back door.

- A check we received from Kerwin Baptist Church covered the total cost of the fluorescent light fixtures for the ceiling of the lounge and dining room.

- One night fifteen men from Gospel Light Baptist Church removed the metal ceiling from the lounge, dining room, and kitchen so that we could replace it with drywall to meet code.

- When we needed a larger electrical panel installed, a young electrician from Kernersville, North Carolina, helped us. Our target opening date, July 22, was fast approaching, the electrical work wasn't finished and we were unsure as to whether our volunteer electrician would have time to come by. Once more God was at work. The young electrician showed up to complete the work before the opening. He told me he had set his alarm clock to get up early for an out-of-town job. Sometime during the night his pet skunk pushed the button that turned off the alarm. Since he didn't have time to get to that job, the young man came to the Mission to finish his work for us — we had electricity in time for our opening service. In remembering the story of that skunk, I have often said, "If the Lord could use a stinker like that, surely He can use each of us if we will only yield our lives to Him."

In a little more than seven weeks, we were ready to have our opening service on July 22, 1967. Everything was ready except we were without running water in the kitchen that day. Fortunately, we didn't need to use the kitchen. Paul Meyers Bar-B-Que catered our opening dinner, and we used paper plates. Our special guests were Dr. Gilbert Stenholm from BJU, Rev. Wayman Pritchard, and the Winston-Salem Police Chief, Justice Tucker. Rev. Pritchard, who became my mentor, had worked at several missions and established the Raleigh Rescue Mission in 1961. As an encouragement to me to follow God's leading, he advised me, "A gnat can eat an elephant if he takes small bites and comes back often enough."

First Mission on Trade Street

It was exciting to see how the Lord was answering our prayers. The vision I had been sharing with people in Winston-Salem for only fifty-two days was fast becoming a reality: "Food for the hungry, rest for the weary, clothes for the needy, and Christ for the sinner." As I look back, I realize what a miracle it was to start with a vision on June 1, 1967, and to be open and ready on July 22 to offer the services I had on my heart for hurting men. Someone once said, "If you can explain everything that has happened in your life, you have lived a man-centered and controlled life, but if there are things and times with no human explanation, perhaps God has shown He is sufficient." The Bible tells us, "I can do all things through Christ which strengtheneth me." (Phil. 4:13) There was much more I would learn about our miraculous God through the experiences of the next thirty-three years.

7

A GROWING MINISTRY

———————◆———————

A few days before we opened, a homeless man named
Joe came to the Mission. I witnessed to him and
talked with him at length. Joe was a great help with the last
minute preparations for the Mission opening. (We had actu-
ally kept seven men overnight before we officially opened,
one of whom trusted Christ as Savior.) One morning I went
to see Joe but found only a note that read, "Thanks for letting me stay with you. I feel my work is done now that the
Mission is open. By the time you get this note, I will be on
my way to my next destination." Joe was among the first
to enter the Mission, but, over the years, thousands more in
need would come and find a warm welcome and a genuine
desire to meet their spiritual and physical needs.

Based on information I gathered from other rescue missions, I developed an interview procedure for checking a
man into the Mission. Every man who came in was counseled personally to ensure he heard the plan of salvation
clearly and was given the opportunity to accept Christ. If
he was not ready at that time, we had prayer and then gave
him the rules to read and sign to indicate he would abide by
them. If he could not read, I read them to him. We assigned
him a bed, fed him, and gave him the opportunity to take

a shower and receive clean clothes. We assured him we would do everything we could to help him physically and spiritually. Every man had a story to tell — what happened that caused him to become homeless and his most pressing problem at the time. Most men would talk freely with me, and I truly enjoyed hearing their stories and learning about their lives. I wanted them to understand that at the Mission we had a deep desire to know them and help them put their lives back together through the love of Christ.

I had a weekly broadcast on a local radio station, and the local newspaper widely publicized our Mission opening and our ministry. Within a few weeks, we had as many as ten clients. For the first few weeks, Barbara prepared meals for the men. Barbara was balancing a full-time job at the radio station, managing our home, and cooking meals for the Mission, which consumed a considerable amount of her time. However, we soon had a cook come in to prepare the meals — a blessing for Barbara. I was amazed by how the Lord was not only supplying the food, but also how He was bringing men in from the streets, men who shared their talents with us in return for the message they needed to hear and the care we offered them. We were living by faith and trusting our Heavenly Father to send men with whom I could share the Gospel and help them to become responsible God-fearing citizens when they left the Mission.

Because rescue missions are usually located in "less desirable" neighborhoods where children desperately need spiritual guidance, it is not unusual to have a children's outreach program. Since I had experience with the Child Evangelism Fellowship ministry, from that first summer of 1967 until 1970, we held a Sunday afternoon service in the Mission chapel for the local children. Students from what was then Piedmont Bible College helped us gather the neighborhood children and bring them to the service.

Eventually, we had so many children we had to borrow a bus from Salem Baptist Church to bring them to the Mission. That first summer nine children made a profession of faith. However, as the number of men at the Mission grew, we did not have room for the forty or so children who came for Sunday afternoon service. My good friends Don and Shirley Collier, who worked with Child Evangelism Fellowship, came to Winston-Salem and took over the children's ministry.

Neighborhood Children

I learned very quickly that the men needed something to do with their time. My grandmother taught me at an early age the old adage, "Idle hands are the Devil's workshop." Chores around the Mission were the same as around any home — someone had to keep the building clean, do laundry, wash dishes, and take out the trash. Additionally, I needed someone to answer the phone and someone to be a night watchman. I created a jobs list from which I assigned jobs to every able-bodied man who came into the Mission.

They saw me doing the menial jobs. So, as long as I was willing to work, I felt comfortable asking them to help. I never asked them to do a job I wasn't willing to do. Most of the men wanted something to do until they could find a job in the community. They wanted to help me reach out to other men, men living like they had been living before coming to the Mission. I did my best to show them appreciation and compliment them on having done a good job. This simple acknowledgement of their efforts encouraged them and gave them a sense of accomplishment, something they needed to rebuild their self-esteem. Some of the men found outside jobs, but wanted to stay at the Mission until they were confident in their faith in Christ and in their own sobriety. Generally, these men paid rent until they had saved enough money to move out on their own.

As the word spread about the ministry of the Mission, we received ever increasing donations of food, clothing, furniture and appliances. Because of the community's generosity, I had to find storage space for the growing number of donations. As a short-term solution, I secured the use of an empty building next door. As the building reached its storage capacity, I didn't know what I was going to do. I did not want to turn away the gifts the Lord's people sent to us. God's blessings had presented me with a problem. However, through the problems God gave me, I learned to seek His wisdom to solve them according to His will.

Approximately two months after we opened the Mission, an older man living at the Mission told me he once had managed a store for a ministry. That statement provided the answer for my storage problem. I located an old, empty building in the 1200 block of North Trade Street, four blocks from the Mission, which was made available to the Mission without charge. We borrowed a truck and hauled the furnishings to our first store. I set my friend up with a table and a chair in front of the only door to the store, gave him a few dollars to make change, and we were in business. Within six weeks, we made six hundred dollars and considerably reduced our inventory. We also gave items to needy families who came to the Mission asking for help. My vision for the Mission to minister to all those in need was being realized. God had provided the answer to my dilemma of what to do with the abundance He had provided through his people.

I didn't have money in our budget to hire help, and keeping my finger on all the Lord had given me to manage became quite a challenge. Every Friday, I gave the men who helped at the Mission some money. It wasn't much, but it helped them buy personal items. We generated a special spirit at the Mission as we worked together to help each other. When I talked to the men about their experiences staying in other missions and how those missions operated, they were eager to tell me how they had been treated. Every man who came into the Mission taught me something—if nothing else but patience. I was not only eager to hear their ideas, but also to implement some of those ideas to improve the management of the Mission. In this way, the men recognized that they were contributing to the success of the ministry. I believed that if they abided by the rules, went to morning devotions, attended evening services, and received my counseling, such exposure to the Word of God could forever change their lives.

I was constantly involved in some facet of the ministry—supervising the Mission, counseling the men, doing the purchasing, and managing the men who ran the store during the day. I visited churches during the evenings and spoke wherever there was an opportunity to share my vision for the Mission. Fortunately, local pastors and laymen came to the Mission and were the missionaries throwing out the lifeline of salvation in every evening service. They spoke to the men about how to get to Heaven when they died and how to live on this earth while they lived. We had six evening services a week as well as daily morning devotions. I conducted Sunday morning services at 9 a.m. I used this time to speak to the men about what was on my heart for them. Sometimes I would speak at an 11 a.m. Sunday service of a local church. Many churches also called me to speak on Wednesday nights. Often, one of the men from the Mission who had received Christ would accompany us to give his testimony.

Not long after the Mission opened a small, frail man came by and introduced himself saying, "My name is Floyd Brown. I think you know two of my sons, Henry and Jerry."

Henry and Jerry Brown had worked with me in the Dining Common at BJU. Their family was known as the Singing Brown Family. Preacher Brown, as he was affectionately known, became my most available and dedicated volunteer. He was a great piano player and loved to preach, pray, or witness. He fell in love with the Rescue Mission

Preacher Floyd Brown

ministry. Preacher Brown was disabled, but he came to the Mission whenever he felt like it and did what he could. For the first year, he was the only help I had to support the evening services. Those times when I was invited to speak at a local church's evening service, he was the one man I could count on to cover the services at the Mission. After Preacher Brown passed away, his son Henry told me that he believed his dad lived longer because he loved to come to the Mission and help in the ministry.

I always tried to have a member of the Mission staff at each service to introduce the speakers. Unfortunately, the speaker would sometimes forget to come. One particular night when I was to be that staff member, the speaker did not show up. I had to think of a message while I was leading the singing. God put the right message on my heart because, when I gave the invitation, two of the six men attending the service accepted Christ as their Savior.

* * *

A Life Reclaimed

Once when I visited a local church, a lady who had been waiting for me in the church foyer asked me if I was the minister with the Rescue Mission. When I answered yes, she told me she was the daughter of Brockley Rodgers and asked if I remembered when he stayed at the Mission. She was surprised that I remembered him. I was just as surprised to meet the daughter of a man I had led to the Lord shortly after the Mission opened in 1967. She listened intently as I recalled how her Dad had come to the Rescue Mission.

Brockley came into the Mission from among the kudzu vines along the railroad tracks where he was living and drinking 'squeeze,' the product of Sterno™ strained through a cloth. After several weeks, he approached me in the chapel and said he wanted to visit his mother. But, before he left, he wanted to get his heart right with the Lord. We prayed together in the prayer room, where he asked the Lord into his heart. Afterwards he said, "I am ready to go see Mom now." When he recovered from his addiction, Brockley asked me if I would help him get his job back as an inhalation therapist in the local hospital. I assured him I would do my best to help.

Several months later I was visiting my wife and our new baby girl, Beverly, at Forsyth Memorial Hospital in Winston-Salem. Surprisingly, I heard this intercom announcement, "Brockley Rodgers, Brockley Rodgers would you come to the Inhalation Therapy Department please." They were calling for the services of the man we ministered to some months back. (I later heard he started an Inhalation Therapy Department in Lexington, North Carolina.)

Brockley's daughter was overjoyed to hear the story of his conversion. She told me that, at a time when he was hospitalized for several weeks, she and her mother, fearing the end was near, asked him about his salvation. He assured them he was ready to meet his Lord. Brockley never recovered physically; but, more importantly, he never recanted his faith in his Lord Jesus Christ.

8

A WARM HEART AND
A TOUGH HIDE

———————◆———————

While working in the store kept the men busy, the sales helped pay expenses for the Mission. A mere six weeks after we opened the store, I was disheartened when I received notification from the authorities that our building had been condemned and was scheduled for demolition. We had to vacate. There is a saying, "If God closes one door He will open another." I prayed He would open the door to another location for our store—He did.

Foss Smithdeal, owner and manager of Smithdeal Reality, rented us his store-front building, just two blocks south of the Mission, at 706 North Trade Street for seventy-five dollars a month. He liked our idea and believed we would succeed. He became a good friend and supporter of the Mission ministry.

We moved our merchandise into the new place and opened the new store on September 12, 1967. In big red letters, the sign above the door read, "Mission Outlet." The new location was much better than our first. We had a bathroom, a front and back door, and a donated heater to ward off the coming winter's chill. Someone donated a cash register and a counter on which to set it. We were ready for business!

The workings of the Lord in the life of our Mission continued to be nothing short of miraculous.

- We needed a truck to pick up donated furniture and major appliances. Someone gave us an old Volkswagen bus (a van-type vehicle) that we used until someone else gave us a 1952 Chevrolet pickup truck.
- Some of the donated appliances needed to be repaired before we could put them in the store. A man came to stay in the Mission who could repair major appliances.
- An electrician who had fallen on hard times checked into the Mission. He put electrical outlets on the walls so we could display and demonstrate refrigerators, stoves, and clothes dryers. We also had outlets in the back of the store to test washing machines for customers.

In those early months I was learning how to minister to these men, but I was by no means "street smart." Sometime in the early fall a belligerent, intoxicated man caused problems. Following evening services, I retired to our upstairs apartment for the day. Soon, the man I had left in charge called and told me a troublemaker was in the lobby. I immediately went downstairs to resolve the situation. The minute he saw me the troublemaker threw a punch at me. He was five inches taller and fifty pounds heavier than I. I ducked the punch and grabbed him around the waist, his head drooping over my shoulder. Claude Coltrane and Raleigh Meyers, two elderly men who had been with us for awhile, came to my aid. Although both men had health problems, they managed to take down my attacker and end the altercation. The man staggered to his feet and left. The next day I found a hole in the nylon sweater I had been wearing where my attacker had drooled on me. I had no way of knowing what he drank that caused the hole, but I kept that sweater to remind me how the Lord protected me through Claude and Raleigh. I knew I had earned the men's respect when they did not hesitate to come to my defense.

By September, at least fifteen men had come to us. A sense of self-worth and appreciation as understood through God's love were important encouragements if they were going to stay with us, remain sober, and hear the life-changing Word of God. Claude reminded me of how important that was. Claude, who came from Pulaski, Virginia, stayed at the Mission and managed our store for several years. Once, as we were walking down the street he said, "Preacher, you don't know what it means to me just to hold my head up and walk down the street with you." I had the opportunity to visit Claude's family in Pulaski and, years later, was asked to preach his funeral.

Word of the new Mission in Winston-Salem quickly spread through "the grapevine" among the homeless. With each passing day and with every new man who sought refuge in the Mission my responsibilities increased, and so did my prayers for wisdom. James 1:5 tells us, "If any of you lack wisdom, let him ask of God, that giveth to all men liberally; and upbraideth not; and it shall be given him."

I heard it said, "To operate a rescue mission you need a warm heart and a tough hide." I asked the Lord to fill me with a compassionate love for these men and promised I would treat every man as I would want my dad to be treated if he came to the Mission. I wanted to show them God's unconditional, all-encompassing love. Even though a special bond developed between the men and me, they understood that they had to keep the rules. For instance, if they drank intoxicants I asked them to leave. Sometimes, knowing we were short on manpower, a man who held an "important" job, such as cook or truck driver, would test me to see if I'd make him leave. I did. He needed to know we trusted the Lord to meet our needs and not man alone. I had to show character and fairness, so I prayed for wisdom regularly. I told those who broke the rules, "You are just as good as anybody else in the Mission, but you are not any better. You can come back in two weeks if you like." It was amazing how many were glad to get back into the Mission as soon as they could.

Through the Lord's leading, I was learning much from our clients. I listened to their stories, got to know them, and tried to understand their addictive tendencies. I grew spiritually as I ministered to the homeless. While some men accepted the philosophy and genuine concern that was present in the Mission, others did not. My personal attitude could bring out the best or the worst in a man. Sometimes you have to win a person to yourself before you can win him to Christ. I did what I promised, and I expected them to do the same for the Mission. When asked what they liked about our Mission, the men usually said the food, the opportunity to work, and the staff. My desire was for them to realize that, if they trusted in the Lord, He would work in their lives as He did in mine.

At times, I was so focused on the physical and spiritual needs of the men I did not notice other needs for the Mission. However, the Lord always stands ready to provide for those who trust and serve Him through people with a charitable spirit and a loving heart. For instance, while touring the building, Mrs. Mary Bird noticed the poor condition of the lobby's floor tile. Afterward, she bought us new vinyl tile and Glen Bass, owner and manager of Salem Tile Company, installed it. We were fortunate to become one of Mrs. Bird's favorite charities.

Some special friends of the Mission who provided produce and groceries, and helped in other ways were: David Byrd, who worked at E. G. Forest Produce Company; Herman Collins and his son-in-law, Joe Choplin, who owned and managed Collins Grocery Store; and W.G. White and his nephew, Doug White, who owned and managed W. G. White Grocery Store. These were well-established and respected businesses that operated for years within a few blocks of the Mission. Occasionally, they hired men who were ready to work outside the Mission. One such man, Walter Green, was hired by E. G. Forest. Five years later, Walter was chosen employee of the year and received special recognition from Jeff Holderfield, the company president.

In time, I understood that while people may like what you are doing for the homeless, they don't want it done in their neighborhood. So, these good neighbors and friends who actively supported the Mission were assuredly among God's blessings on our ministry. Having a good relationship with my neighbors was a tremendous encouragement. We expressed our sincerest appreciation through written letters to all who supported us in any way as we endeavored to establish a mission to minister to the less fortunate in our city. More importantly, I thanked God for His provision. Philippians 4:19 reads, "But my God shall supply all your need according to his riches in glory by Christ Jesus."

9

UNDER THE PROTECTION OF ANGELS

---◦---

Winston-Salem was not spared the civil unrest and race riots that rocked our nation during the 1960s. On the morning of November 2, 1967, riots started downtown and spread to East Winston by evening. The Mission was located well within the target area of the rioters.

Brother Joe Franklin, a lay preacher, finished the evening service, which focused on Exodus 12:13, "...and when I see the blood, I will pass over you...." One of the men brought me a message that there had been some rioting in sections of Winston-Salem. I finished my work downstairs and made sure the doors were locked before going upstairs to Barbara. She had heard the news on television. She also heard that people were warned to stay home. We did not know what would happen in our skid row neighborhood.

We lived in the rear apartment, but the front apartment was empty so we could see the street in front. We stood in the dark and watched as a group of rioters gathered at the corner of North Trade and Ninth Street. As the crowd continued to grow, the noise level increased. Then suddenly, approximately seventy-five men carrying sticks and rocks charged across the street toward the Mission. Our ministry was less than six-months old. Barbara and I were still new-lyweds — who at that moment feared for our physical well-being. We watched and prayed trusting wholly in God's protection. The rioters threw rocks through the large windows of the Army-Navy Surplus Store next door and looted it. They also threw "fire bombs" into the building that fortunately did not ignite. I will never forget seeing the angry mob rushing across the street. I thought of the angry mob the Bible tells of in Luke 23:21 that yelled to Pontius Pilot, "Crucify him, Crucify him," concerning Jesus' Crucifixion. We had no way of knowing if they were going to break the large windows of the Mission. As the message of Exodus 12:13 preached earlier that night had told of the Lord's protection of the Israelites, I can only believe it was by God's hand the mob passed by us.

The police responded to our report of the incident, but the mob disappeared down the alleys until the police left. Then they would return to continue looting. This went on throughout the night. The next day things quieted down, but we were apprehensive about what nightfall would bring. Thankfully, as the evening approached, we noticed an armed National Guardsman standing across the street. Several years later when we were visiting a local church, a young man came up to me and introduced himself as the National Guardsman who had guarded us that night. I thanked him and told him how much better we felt having him out there. Interestingly enough, he told me he did not have ammunition in his weapon.

There was restlessness in our neighborhood for months. Consequently, we established a plan requiring a police escort for any large group of men seeking admission to the Mission. We knew that the people who had genuine needs would be glad to cooperate. While the police occasionally brought someone to us, they never did bring a group.

The rioting that began on November 2 finally ended on November 7 when the Governor mobilized the National Guard. Businesses in Winston-Salem suffered more than one million dollars in damages, and more than one hundred and ninety-two rioters were arrested. Through it all, God's Rescue Mission was spared and continued to minister to the lost and hurting men seeking shelter within its walls. The Lord blessed us through those trying times and spared us from the unrest and disturbance going on around us, for which we were forever thankful. The Bible tells us in Psalms 91:10-11, 10"there shall no evil befall thee, neither shall any plague come nigh thy dwelling. 11For he shall give his angels charge over thee, to keep thee in all thy ways."

10

FIRST CHRISTMAS AT THE MISSION

In just a few months, the Mission received an ever growing number of men, which added significantly to our operating costs. We needed more food, the cooler temperatures of fall added heating costs that carried through winter, and I needed more help to supervise the men. Since this was our first year in operation, we had no financial data against which we could gauge how much costs might increase. We had come this far by faith and there was no reason to think our Lord would fail us now.

Barbara and I knew these lost souls were overlooked and turned away by the world around them. They had little, if any, contact with the family and friends they knew before their addictions. We wanted them to understand that, no matter their previous circumstance, they were loved by God and the people He sent to minister to them. Making a man feel at "home" in an institutional setting is a daunting challenge, but one that we prayed we could accomplish. We thought of things that would make them feel special, things that they missed while estranged from their family.

We decided to serve a monthly cake to celebrate the birthdays of each of the men whose birthdays fell in that month. They appreciated our recognition of their special day. Since this was our first Thanksgiving and Christmas with them, we wanted to provide an experience that would remind them of the good things from their past holidays. We prepared a special Thanksgiving dinner with all the trimmings. We had an abundance of food, so we invited all the street people to dinner as Christ instructs in Luke 14:13, "But when thou makest a feast, call the poor, the maimed, the lame, the blind:" Barbara and I felt blessed to share the meal with the men. Our experience in preparing Thanksgiving taught us how to better prepare for Christmas.

We held our Christmas party on the evening of December 19, the Tuesday before Christmas. While most of them were destitute, the men somehow scraped up enough money to buy Barbara and me a five-pound box of candy and some bathroom towels. They also bought a cake inscribed with the passage from Matthew 25:35, "For I was an hungered and ye gave me meat: I was thirsty, and ye gave me drink: I was a stranger, and ye took me in:" It was so pretty we did not cut it for several days. Their gift demonstrated a heartfelt appreciation that touched us deeply.

That first Christmas several friends from outside the Mission joined us to celebrate our Lord's birthday. Among them were Preacher Floyd and Mrs. Agnes Brown and Jean Upchurch. We had no idea that several years later Jean's ex-husband Bobby Upchurch would be a client at the Mission, or that two of her sons would serve on our staff.

Just before Christmas day, Claude Coltrane, the elderly man who previously helped subdue the troublemaker in the lobby, was talking with a visitor. Claude told of how his original intent was to beat the Mission out of a couple of nights lodging, but surprisingly he found himself staying on to help Preacher Wilcox fix the place as a refuge for men—mostly alcoholics—who had no place to go. Sober now, he said he did not have to stay at the Mission. His family in Virginia was amazed at the change in him and would welcome him home. He could have spent Christmas there if he wished. He said he wanted to stay at the Mission though because he saw the need to help others for Christmas.

Claude reminisced how, when he was a young boy, Christmas was happy time—a family time during which his mother prepared oysters. He spoke of the stockings filled with presents for the nine children in the family and fondly remembered the Christmas he received a pair of wooden horses that were mounted on rockers with a seat between them. He described how thirty years ago, before he became an alcoholic, he had his own children with whom he celebrated a happy Christmas. But, when alcohol changed his life, he wandered the countryside—sometimes working, sometimes in jail, much of the time drunk.

He told the visitor that apparently the word was out about the Mission. In the five months since it had opened, one hundred and eighty-five men from twenty-two states had passed through the Mission's doors. Once they had a couple of good meals under their belt and could loosen it up a notch or two, most of them kept on going. Claude said, "The good cooking is the reason so many men are coming to the Mission; and, if Preacher Wilcox doesn't get rid of that cook, every bum in the country will show up here."

If good food was what was bringing men to the Mission where their bodies and souls could be nourished, then Abbot Wilson, our cook, was another of God's blessings to our ministry. At one time, Abbot had a family, children, and a good job in a restaurant. Before coming to the Mission, he lost it all to his addiction. So, while Christmas 1967 may have seemed like just another day for Abbot, he didn't realize he was one of the most appreciated men at the Mission.

December 25, 1967, was our first of many Christmases we spent with those the Lord sent in from the streets.

11

THE BLESSING OF
BROTHER MILLS

We made it through that first winter with the help of the Lord and our supporters. The racial unrest that plagued Winston-Salem in November 1967 had settled down. But, following the service on April 4, 1968, we heard the news that Dr. Martin Luther King, Jr. had been shot. Barbara was almost six months pregnant, and our memories of the November riots were still very vivid. Apprehensive about what might happen and concerned for Barbara's safety, we decided it best to stay with friends that night. I instructed the night watchman as to what to do and gave him a telephone number where he could reach me should problems arise. Fortunately, all went well at the Mission that night, and he did not have to call. Barbara and I returned the next morning.

Knowing the homeless would be fed, have a clean place to stay, and hear the Word of God encouraged the community to send them to the Mission, rather than give them money or handouts. We stenciled our message of "Food for the hungry, Rest for the weary, Clothes for the needy, and Christ for the sinners" on our trucks for all to see as the trucks picked up donations. In searching for a way to expand our pickup services, we found a market for old newspapers. We picked them up with our regular donations, tied them in bundles, and sold them for a penny a pound. It didn't sound like much, but people literally saved tons of newspapers and gladly gave them to us. We used the earnings from their discarded papers to restore the lives of discarded men.

An elderly friend, Henry Smith, drove a donated 1951 Chevrolet one and a half ton, green panel truck (nicknamed "the green hornet") on our newspaper runs to High Point, North Carolina. For each load of 10,000 pounds delivered, we received one hundred dollars. Each time I paid Henry ten dollars for driving the truck and supervising the men to unload it, the Mission received ninety dollars. We set collection goals for the year and generated enthusiasm in the community to help us by saving their newspapers. In the spring of 1968, we were then able to project to our donors that, if they continued to save their papers for us, we could hire another staff member with the income generated.

Later, we learned to take salvage items from donors — scrap metal, rags, and later cardboard from grocery stores — and sell them to help us salvage precious souls. A friend once told me, "You use our discards to rejuvenate social rejects."

In hopes of getting a young man to come to Winston-Salem that summer and help me at the Mission, I contacted students who would be completing their training at BJU at the end of the spring semester. Ernest Mills, a student from Greenville, North Carolina, talked with me about coming to live at the Mission. With our baby due in July, Barbara and I felt Brother Mills was an

Rev. Ernie Mills

answer to our prayer. Since we wanted to move out of our apartment at the Mission before the baby came, Brother Mills could take care of things at night because he would be on-site. He understood his salary was based on the sale of old papers. We agreed he'd start at one hundred and fifty dollars a month plus room and board. Brother Mills has often teased me about the fact he did not get a raise when income from paper sales increased to four hundred dollars a month.

Brother Mills and I were naturals to work together; our life experiences were so similar. He came from a farming background, and his dad was an alcoholic who died when Ernie was young. Ernie had to work while he was in high school to help his mom and his siblings, and then had to work his way through college. His genuine compassion for the men and his strong work ethic were obvious. When I gave him his job description and he understood his responsibilities, he wondered how I had managed to cover it all before he came. It was wonderful to work with a like-minded young man with the same passionate desire as me to serve the Lord.

Barbara and I had been at the Mission one year when Brother Ernie came. We had been open a little over ten months and statistics showed that by June 30, 1968, we had assisted 464 men; given 14,534 meals to the hungry; provided 5,228 nights lodging to weary bodies; and distributed an unknown quantity of clothing to the needy. We had conducted five hundred services and had sixty professions of faith and rededications. All our bills were paid on time and we rejoiced in the goodness of our Lord.

With the prospect of Brother Ernie living at the Mission, Barbara and I had to find a house in the short time remaining before our baby arrived. We had planned for unexpected expenses, but had not expected them to be so much. The Lord was completely sufficient for the needs of the Mission—now we were asking him to meet our special need. I learned when you pray for help in an uncertain situation, it is important to ask the Lord to help you bring glory and honor to Him in resolving the difficulty.

By now I had made many friends in a number of churches. I mentioned our need to a Christian friend, Gail Lyons, a contractor who knew several real estate agents. I explained that we needed a mortgage payment that included interest, insurance and taxes, and was within our means. Based on our income, it was a bold request. Gail soon called to say he had found us a house west of Winston-Salem in a development called Somerset. After we had seen the house, we prayed about it before we called him back to get more information. Gail told us we could assume the loan on the house and the all-inclusive payment would be within our budget. While that sounded good, it didn't include the down payment. Mr. Lyons, my dear friend, blessed us by working with the seller to apply his finder's fee as the down payment. Once again I remembered Rev. Pritchard's words, "God will always pay for what He orders." By the grace of God, we were able to move in and decorate a room for our little baby. God is good all the time!

July 8, 1968, I was at the Mission covering a service that night. Barbara was home baking a cake for the night watchman, Clyde Branch, whose birthday was the next day. After the service ended and the visiting preacher left, I checked with the men to see that everything was under control. Then Barbara called me and told me it was time for her to go to the hospital. All signs were go, and I needed to come home immediately. I briefed the night watchman and left to take her to the hospital. But, before I left, Clyde reminded me his birthday was the next day, and he hoped the baby would not come until after midnight. Once Barbara was admitted, the nurses told me to go home and they would call me later. I returned home praying that all would go well with Barbara and the baby. It was about 9:30 p.m. when I got home. I thought of Barbara. We had been married five years, and even though I did not know what might happen that night, I knew it would change the rest of our lives. I thought how much I loved her and remembered how I had worked night and day to get the Mission open and operating. During the eleven months we lived over the Mission, I had eaten supper with my wife and spent the evening with her only six times. I, like so many men, was so completely absorbed in my work I neglected the love of my life. I found out after we moved into our house that she had often been upstairs feeling lonely while I was downstairs taking care of the needs of the men. She never complained. I was ashamed of myself for my insensitivity to her needs. Yes, the Lord gave me a good talking to that night, and I never forgot it! I thanked the Lord for his good grace in giving me a very special wife. It was then that the phone rang. The nurse called to update me that Barbara was doing fine. At 11:30 p.m. I got a call to come to the hospital.

I ran out the door—but where was my car? I knew I had parked it in the driveway. It was then I saw it across the street sitting beside the fire hydrant. Apparently, I had forgotten to put the car in park, and it had drifted across the street. Thank the Lord it missed the fire hydrant and sustained no damage. I drove to Forsyth Memorial Hospital, went to the waiting room and gave the nurse my wife's name. At 11:50 p.m. our little Beverly was born. Mom and baby did great!

It was very special now to come home and see Barbara and little Beverly. With Brother Mills staying at the Mission, I could be home two or three nights a week with my wife and baby. Yes, life was quite different now. I learned that the director of a mission should not live on the property any longer than necessary, especially if he is married and has a family. God placed these two gentle, beautiful people in my life and had just reminded me I needed to give them as much time as I could.

* * *

God brought Brother Ernie and me together for His purpose. Brother Ernie was my first male staff member and, without question, the right man for the job. He stayed and worked with me for five and a half years. He met his wife, Gail Gerrey, when she came with her church youth group to conduct a service at the Mission. Ernie and Gail were married in August 1969 at Crestview Baptist Church, one of our supporting churches. On a trip to visit family in Greenville, the Lord laid Durham, North Carolina, on Brother Ernie's heart. It took several months before he responded to the Lord's call and moved his wife and little boy to Durham to start a rescue mission. His wonderful book, *A Step of Faith: The History of the Durham Rescue Mission*, chronicles the story of the mission he established in November 1974. Over the last forty years, the Mills have done an amazing work for the Lord in their ministry. Recently, the Durham Rescue Mission completed a new Men's Division, fully paid for by the time it was dedicated. The women and children also have a beautiful facility. By the grace of our good God, miracles are taking place at this mission.

Barbara and I try to celebrate all their special occasions with them. We could not be more proud of the Mills. Their son, Ernie Jr., works in the ministry with his father. Their daughter, Bethany, is a registered nurse at Duke University Hospital in Durham. They have three beautiful grandchildren.

12

The Importance of Trust

———•———

With our fledgling year behind us and Ernie Mills to help us, I devoted more time to praying and meditating on the direction in which God wanted me to take the Mission. He showed me that destitute senior men and the disabled in the community needed a permanent place to live where they would be safe from the street life—a place that provided nourishing food and spiritual guidance. But, no matter how we tried to configure the space in our building, it just wasn't enough to accommodate a Senior Division at that time. I concluded that our present building was too small to house the expanded vision God gave me for the ministry. At the same time, I knew if God was in it, He would provide. It was a burden on my heart that was to be fulfilled in God's timing, not mine.

Men were staying with us whose sobriety and in-depth counseling depended upon an extended stay. Some men who were now living clean and sober had no families or were estranged from their family. Others had jobs outside the Mission, but still needed time to grow in their faith before facing temptation in a worldly environment. We wanted them to have every opportunity to succeed. Realizing the value of rewarding the men for making progress in their lives, as an incentive, we renovated some spaces to provide semi-private quarters for them. In the basement, which was set up dormitory style, we divided one side into two small rooms suitable for four men. We renovated the upstairs storage rooms into living quarters. This gave the men with outside jobs a place to prove to themselves the extent of their progress. In providing privacy for them, we were challenged by the limitations of our existing building. Our facilities were old and makeshift, but what we lacked in facilities we made up for with our compassion and commitment to share the Spirit of Christ with every client we were privileged to serve. We placed our full faith and trust in the Lord to provide exactly what we needed, exactly when we needed it. Psalms 9:10 tells us, "And they that know thy name will put their trust in thee: for thou, LORD, hast not forsaken them that seek thee."

Over the next few years, I learned to rely on God's wisdom to perfect my skills in understanding the men who came to us. I knew we would be taken advantage of at times. Anyone who has dealt with street people knows you can sometimes misplace your trust in an individual. Trust is a fragile bond that is easily broken. For the sake of the ministry, it was a constant balance of knowing who to trust and when to trust them. Alcoholics and addicts recognize when someone is suspicion and untrusting of them—ready to accuse them of questionable behavior. Once they sensed this they became resistant to our ministry. Too often, men who were sober and trying to go straight were falsely accused by others of breaking their sobriety. Addictions are a powerful tool in Satan's arsenal. Addicts of any kind will deny their addiction and lie about returning to their old ways. The acquisition of a breathalyzer and drug testing kit helped us better determine those who had broken our trust.

We trusted Mission men to drive our trucks, run our store, and answer our phone. Rarely did we have a problem with stealing. However, occasionally a driver would "steal" a truck. When it happened, we'd report it to the police and pray that we would get it back—we always did. Often the driver would simply use the truck to take himself to another city, park it at the police station, and take the keys inside to the desk clerk. When the police called us, we would go pick it up. Once, we went as far as Jacksonville, Florida.

In the ministry of rescue, we had to trust the Lord every day, all day. Only the Lord can impart the special love needed to work with these men—men who are sometimes called the least, the last, and the lost. As difficult as it seemed for us to trust these men, we tempered that with an understanding that they too did not know whom they could trust. They had been deceived, lied to, cheated and taken advantage of by those they trusted at one time. Hurting people often harbor a lot of bitterness they feel they cannot resolve. This causes them to not trust people or God.

Once we earned their trust and respect, we built a relationship that allowed them to open their heart and unburden the things of their past. This allowed us to assure them Jesus cares and forgives past sin, no matter how bad we think it is, if we confess it to Him and ask His forgiveness. "For all have sinned, and come short of the glory of God." (Rom. 3:23) "If we confess our sins, he is faithful and just to forgive us *our* sins, and to cleanse us from all unrighteousness." (1 John 1:9) "For thou, Lord, *art* good, and ready to forgive; and plenteous in mercy unto all them that call upon thee."(Ps. 86:5)

I have found if we let Christ live through us, reflecting His character and compassion in all we do, and, if we use the Word of God to witness to hurting humanity, the Holy Spirit can make hearts tender and create a desire in those we touch to trust Christ as Savior. I have seen it work!

13

WITH RENEWED PURPOSE

———◦———

The 1970s brought miraculous changes to our growing ministry. But, before any of this happened, God prepared our hearts to receive the special gift He would bestow.

In 1973, Barbara and I attended Bill Gothard's seminar, Institute in Basic Youth Conflicts, in Atlanta, Georgia. Since the Mission was staffed with key people, and Dr. Billy Martin (our pastor) and Mrs. Martin had agreed to keep Beverly, we felt assured things at home would be fine in our absence. That first six years at the Mission, we had worked tirelessly with indigents who had a multitude of physical, emotional, and spiritual needs. But, we had not taken time to refresh ourselves. We needed spiritual renewal. For us, we believed nothing could refresh the spirit like gathering with others, as the people in Nehemiah 8 gathered, to hear the Word of God and search out its meaning in our lives.

Those six days at the seminar were a time of instruction, learning, and reflection on God's Word. We searched the Scriptures to learn what we were doing with our lives that pleased, or displeased, our Father in Heaven. We learned how we could remove those things that kept us from living out God's will in our daily activities.

During this time of searching and reflection, God placed Psalms 139:14 on my heart, "I will praise thee; for I am fearfully and wonderfully made: marvelous are thy works: and that my soul knoweth right well." I never thought of my size as a problem, but I often wondered why God made me this way. I am a man of small stature, 5 feet 5 inches tall with short legs, short arms, small feet, and small hands. Through meditation, this passage revealed many things to me. First, God made me for a special purpose that He knew, and I wanted to find out. He told me to, 7"Ask, and it shall be given you; seek, and ye shall find; knock and it shall be opened unto you: 8For every one that asketh receiveth; and he that seeketh findeth; and to him that knocketh it shall be opened." (Mat. 7:7-8) As I reflected on my life thus far, and those verses, I was confident He had called me to preach and to direct a rescue mission. Second, God knew what size He needed me to be to accomplish what He had called me to do. Third, God led me to understand that, even though I was small in stature, He had provided me with an insight and understanding that allowed me to reach the men to whom I ministered. I was able to relate to these men and demonstrate to them that they were without excuse. He had given me the confidence that allowed me to set forth His vision for the Mission and be worthy of the support of His people. Fourth, God reinforced what I already knew — what He gives you is to be used to His honor and glory; He is the Creator and we are but His creation. All things are from Him and through Him, and we can accomplish nothing without Him. Finally, more than anything I needed to praise Him, because I was fearfully and wonderfully made to accomplish His plan for me.

As the week went on, I felt the Lord working in my life. In the quiet darkness of the early hours of Friday morning, as Barbara lay sleeping, alone with my thoughts I realized I was not always fully submitted to allowing the Lord to direct the ministry. I saw times when I was so anxious about accomplishing my immediate wants and needs for the Mission I didn't diligently seek the Lord's will. That is when I recognized how important this opportunity for spiritual renewal was for me. I became overwhelmed by my need to praise the Lord, to thank Him for my wonderful wife and daughter, for all He had done and was doing at the Mission, and for the privilege to serve Him in the place to which He called me. I thanked Him for my small feet and hands and rededicated them to Him to use as He would. I asked Him to take me, mold me and make me into what He wanted me to be. I acknowledged that I was not my own, but had been bought with a price — "His precious blood." I assured Him my deepest desire was to live for Him alone. At that moment, as I let go of my will and surrendered to His, a peace settled on me and a burden was lifted. The Bible tells us in Romans 12:1-2, 1"…present your bodies a living sacrifice, holy, acceptable unto God, which is your reasonable service….2be ye transformed by the renewing of your mind, that ye may prove what is that good, and acceptable, and perfect, will of God."

Barbara and I returned home refreshed and renewed, eager to get about doing God's work. By the time I returned to work on Monday morning, the Lord had removed all questions from my mind about His plan for me.

14

A BEACON IN THE DARKNESS

The trip to Atlanta was spiritually uplifting, and I was ready to do whatever the Lord asked of me. As soon as I arrived at the Mission Monday morning, the staff told me that Mr. R. P. Reece was trying to contact me. Although the name was unfamiliar, I returned his call that same morning. I know I serve an awesome God, but I was nothing short of amazed at what He did through Mr. Reece. In February 1973, Mr. Reece donated the Lawrence Apartment Building (the former Lawrence Hospital) at 717 Oak Street to the Rescue Mission. The building was just two blocks from our Trade Street location and had seventy-one furnished rooms. Prior to turning the building over to us, Mr. Reece offered to install fire escapes on the ends of the building. He also had an attorney ensure we wouldn't violate zoning or other laws by converting it into a rescue mission. I was so overcome with joy I wept. Through Divine Providence, Mr. Reece donated a building large enough to hold the vision God laid on my heart for a Senior Division, and more! As we sing in the doxology, "Praise God from Whom all Blessings Flow."

We had to ensure the building met all building codes before we could use it. Unfortunately, Brother Moxley was no longer available to help me work with the various inspectors. I met the inspectors on site. As we walked through the second floor of the three-story building, I remarked, "It's going to cost quite a bit of money to get this building up to standard." One of them replied sarcastically, "I think the first thing you need is a case of dynamite," as if to suggest demolition instead of restoration. That is exactly what many people thought of the unfortunate men who frequented "the jungle" beside the Mission—of little value to the world, hardly worth restoring. God saw it differently.

I heard folks in the community were skeptical of the work at the Mission. I knew the world would underestimate what our God could do. However, after nearly seven years in the Mission ministry, trusting the Lord for our daily needs, I had no reservations about trusting Him to provide what we needed now. Jesus said in Mark 10:27, "… With men it is impossible, but not with God: for with God all things are possible."

Redesigning the space in a building this size was a huge challenge. We had three floors of space with stairways and ramps to get from one floor to the other but no elevator. We needed to move walls and reallocate space, plaster and paint the walls, update electrical fixtures and boxes, rewire, replace old plumbing, and install drop ceilings. The estimated cost for just the materials was twenty thousand dollars. Now, more than ever, I felt the importance of remaining close to my Lord, seeking His will and discerning wisdom. I needed to maintain the Mission to His glory and honor while accomplishing the renovation of our future space. I was totally dependent upon Him. All we are and all we have belong to the Lord, and I knew He would bring the help and supplies we needed to fulfill His vision for the ministry.

Through our newsletter, I appealed to our supporting churches and to thousands of friends of the Mission. I explained what we were about to undertake and the vision we had for the added space. We prayed God would speak to the hearts of our friends and help us open the doors to the new building by the fall of 1974. We were absolutely amazed to see how God worked on the hearts of our supporters. We prayed, and the people gave. By this time, we had added several staff members to help with operating the Mission. Nevertheless, the added task of renovating the newly acquired building stressed our manpower to the limit. Besides supervising the recovering men who worked at the Mission, we were making as many as fifty donation pickups five days a week, operating two stores, and feeding and ministering to as many as thirty-five men each night. Nonetheless, we trusted our God to calm the present stresses of life with His peace Isaiah 26:3 reads, "Thou wilt keep him in perfect peace, whose mind is stayed on thee: because he trusteth in thee."

We took things a day at a time and followed the Lord's leading. In 1973 and 1974, it became obvious that the only explanation for our accomplishments was because of the great things our God was doing in the life of the ministry, not because of anything we were doing. We worked on the renovation as God supplied the materials and manpower, but I also ensured that the Gospel was faithfully presented to the men who came to the Mission. Sometimes we put the renovation on hold to make sure we fulfilled what we had committed to doing for the men. Except for hiring a certified electrician to do the electrical work and a company to sandblast the exterior of the building, all the renovations were done by the men who eventually lived there. I believed it gave them a greater appreciation for their future "home" and reinforced their self-esteem when they saw what they could achieve. Years later, men sometimes stopped by the Mission and asked me, "Do you remember me? I helped you renovate this building,"

Before we could move into the new building, we had one last task—install the drop ceilings. I knew nothing about installing them, but what I did know was that if I prayed and asked, the Lord would send the right man at the right time. As it happened, Calvary Baptist Church on Country Club Road was building a multi-million dollar sanctuary, and they were installing a drop ceiling. A man working on their ceiling started drinking alcohol and was relieved of his duties. He came to the Mission, and we helped him get sober. This man helped us install our ceilings, and we moved to our new building in October 1974.

Once again the Lord had shown He is faithful to those who seek His will. What others derided became another opportunity for God to show us His mercy and grace so that He might receive the glory.

Seemingly, Mr. Reece had been motivated to donate his building to us by a kindness shown to his maid by men from the Mission. One day as they were unloading bread for the Mission, they gave her several loaves for her family. Ecclesiastes 11:1 reads, "Cast thy bread upon the waters: for thou shalt find it after many days." Mr. Reece's gift was more than a building—it was the place where we cast the bread of life onto the

Mission Building, 717 Oak Street

waters of the troubled souls who came there and brought so many to a saving knowledge of Jesus Christ.

* * *

In a community whose skyline was adorned with many illuminated crosses, I envisioned one more. A beacon that would guide those in darkness to a place where they could choose to enter the light of God's saving grace. Isaiah 42:16, "And I will bring the blind by a way *that* they knew not; I will lead them in paths *that* they have not known: I will make darkness light before them, and crooked things straight. These things will I do unto them, and not forsake them."

In 1975, the Christian Business Men's Association of Winston-Salem provided and installed atop the Mission a revolving illuminated cross inscribed with "Jesus Saves." The cross lit up the night, reminding the city of the message of God's Rescue Mission. In time, the cross stopped revolving. Because repairs would be costly, we were advised to leave it stationary. Thanks to these good men, as of this writing, the Mission cross still points the lost souls of Winston-Salem to the way, the truth, and the light who is our Lord and Savior, Jesus Christ.

15

SENIOR FOSTER CARE

---◦---

Prior to starting the renovation, I took solitary prayer walks through the building, surveying the available space and pondering where best to locate our Senior Foster Care Division. I decided to locate the ministry on the second floor in eight rooms large enough to accommodate ten men—four men in two semi-private rooms and six in private rooms. They would share common bathroom and shower facilities and a furnished sunroom with a television where they could fellowship. Often taken advantage of by others, these destitute men lived on minimal incomes in squalid conditions. Our door opened for Senior Foster Care Division in October 1974.

Relaxing in the Senior Lounge

Through our ministry, these seniors received their meals and transportation to doctors, Social Services, and Veterans Administration offices. We monitored them daily, and a volunteer nurse came in weekly to consult with them. We counseled with them about spiritual and other concerns, giving them the opportunity to attend evening services. For those who had families, their families could visit. We provided the basics of assisted living to men who otherwise could not make it on their own. The small rent they paid helped cover their expenses, and they had money left over, something to which they weren't accustomed. The Mission was a caring safe haven where they could rest without fear until their health required the more concentrated care provided by a hospital or nursing home. Many times a former client returned to the Mission and entered into our Senior Foster Care Division. The fulfillment of this vision was a miracle to many elderly men who enjoyed their last earthly years with us.

Ladies Division

Having established the Senior Division, we sought the Lord's guidance to identify others in the community to whom we could minister. We soon recognized that the major ministries in the area were serving mostly men, but few were available to serve homeless women. Then, we realized that the Lord had blessed us with the ideal area in our building to respond to this need. Our newly-acquired facility had eight rooms with a private outside entrance and doors that could easily separate and secure that part of the building from the Men's Division. After much prayer and discussion with the Mission Board, we renovated those rooms — the former nurses' quarters of this one-time hospital — into the Ladies' Division in December 1975. Since we needed a live-in attendant for the women, we divided the space into a small, one-bedroom apartment on the first floor, with four bedrooms and two bathrooms upstairs that could accommodate up to ten women. The Lord sent us Miss Margaret Hemric, a qualified lady from one of our supporting churches, to supervise the women and look after the ministry. In addition to managing the Ladies' Division, she also provided some clerical support for the Mission office.

The women were required to follow the same rules as the men. To avoid the potential problems that can arise in this type of close living arrangement, we forbade any physical contact between the men and women and established tight controls to enforce it. The ladies from local churches sometimes conducted a women's Bible study at the Mission. Just as it was important to keep the men busy, the women also needed work. They helped prepare and can vegetables, cooked meals, and sorted clothing donations. Local garment companies sometimes provided piecework and paid the ladies at the Mission to do it. And, like the men, they were allowed to seek outside employment while staying at the Mission.

Some of the women stayed with us awhile and made real progress in their lives. The aunt of a county commissioner stayed with us, and he was very pleased with the way we worked with her. Tina Tate, whose husband Archie was in the Men's Division, stayed with us several years. She often helped Miss Hemric. Later, she and her husband were given an apartment at the Mission until they got their own place. As a rule, we required couples who came to us to live in their respective gender quarters. The Tates were the only couple to ever have an apartment in the Mission.

Until her health no longer permitted, Miss Hemric was dedicated to our Women's ministry. After she left, we were helped by students from Piedmont Bible College. Doris Adegboye from Africa and Cindy Blood Peters from Alaska were two outstanding young women who helped. Our women's ministry lasted for approximately ten years. At a time when homeless women had limited access to rescue shelters, our small ministry brought women to Christ and changed their lives. Then, the Salvation Army built a large new building just down the street from our Mission to serve the needs of women and mothers with children. So, as women's ministries expanded within other community organizations, we closed our Ladies' Division and referred women to those organizations.

As our men's ministry continued to grow, along with its need for more space, we used the former women's quarters for the men. Some men commonly needed to stay with us longer to become firmly rooted in the Word of God, and not fall back into their previous condition when faced with the challenges of living on their own. We formed a Mission Fellowship and an Overcomers group to teach the men how to deal with their addictions and trust the Lord to give them victory and joy in their new life in Christ. We changed the name of the former women's quarters to Bethel Hall and used it as an incentive to encourage life-saving changes in the men. Proverbs 12:14 reads, "A man shall be satisfied with good by the fruit of *his* mouth: and the recompense of a man's hands shall be rendered unto him." Men who earned a significant level of trust deserved an opportunity to have more privacy and were allowed to live there.

16

Beginning a Farm Ministry

---·---

The testimony of a saved person whose heart is devoted to the Lord and whose life reflects it is a powerful tool in reaching the discarded souls of our society. As the speaker for our tenth anniversary, Rev. John Horan gave such a testimony. He told of his life of crime in the mafia, which resulted in him serving seven years in a penitentiary. Then he related his wonderful salvation experience in the rescue mission in Newark, New Jersey. Following his salvation, Rev. Horan devoted his life to serving the Lord. Eventually, he became director of the Orlando Union Rescue Mission in Orlando, Florida, where he served for eighteen years. During his visit, we also went to local Christian schools where he delivered his powerful message to the young people.

Our tenth year presented me with yet another opportunity to expand the ministry in a way I had not imagined. I thought that when I had left my home in Kinston to attend BJU my farming days were behind me. The Lord had other plans.

H. E. Holder donated an apartment building in the Ardmore section of Winston-Salem to the Mission. Zoning laws for the area prevented our using it for the Mission, so a friend offered to take the apartment building as partial payment for a twenty-seven acre farm in Davie County. After much prayer and consultation, we came to believe this was an opportunity to expand our work program and provide food for the Mission. The farm along the Yadkin River had fenced pasture, a small barn, and equipment shed — but no house, equipment, or livestock. While I didn't yet have a plan, I had a vision for the ministry potential of the farm with which the Lord had blessed us. I was up to the challenge — after all, wasn't farming the first job God gave man? Genesis 1:15 says, "And the LORD God took the man, and put him into the garden of Eden to dress it and to keep it." I trusted the Lord.

When I mentioned the acquisition of the farm in our Mission newsletter, two friends gave us two young heifers. Then, our farm neighbors gave us several pigs. Since we didn't have equipment to cultivate the land, we leased it to a neighbor that first year. Eventually, we obtained a John Deere 1020 tractor, a disk, a cultivator, and a breaking plow. By the second year, we were ready to raise corn to feed the animals and vegetables to feed the men. We raised okra, corn, tomatoes, cantaloupes and other fresh vegetables that supplied the Mission, and we also sold some in the Mission store. The land was fertile and our harvest bountiful. Through His blessing, the Lord provided so much more than the few tomatoes we grew in the limited open space around the Mission.

Men from the Mission drove to the farm every day to feed and care for the livestock. Grocery stores saved vegetable trimmings in large metal drums and the Winston-Salem bread companies and local bakeries gave us old bread, which our men collected and fed to the livestock. Twice a week I worked for half a day with the men on the farm. We used donated salvaged lumber to build hog pens, hay feeders for the cows, corrals, loading chutes, and, eventually, a barn in which to store hay. Besides vegetables, we raised and sold grain-fed, custom-cut beef and custom-cut pork. The livestock also provided meat for the Mission, meals for the needy and, for several years, the staff received a quarter-side of beef and half a hog from the farm.

Some of the men really enjoyed getting out of the city to a more peaceful setting. From early childhood, I found that one of the best places to commune with God is outdoors. As I look back, I must admit starting the farm was a very bold move that required me to push my time and energy to a higher level. However, it soon became a place where I recharged my batteries—a place away from everyday clamor where I could listen for the still, small voice of God.

A friend donated a mobile home to us, which we planned to set up on the farm as a place the farm workers from the Mission could stay if needed. Once we relocated the unit to the farm, I contacted Duke Power to install electricity. But the neighbor, whose property our power line had to cross, refused us permission to cross his land. Without electricity, we could not use the mobile home. As time passed, we waited with prayerful patience, allowing God to work. Psalms 27:14 tells us, "Wait on the LORD; be of good courage...." As it turned out, our contrary neighbor was well along in the construction of a new house when a Duke Power worker pointed out that the house was underneath a power line, which was not permissible. He informed our neighbor he would either have to tear down his house, or get our permission to run his power line across our farm. Needless to say, we arrived at a mutual agreement concerning the power lines. Our God is great!

A couple from Piedmont Bible College lived in the mobile home and helped care for the animals. Eventually, we selected a trustworthy man who knew farming to live there. We installed a telephone so I could keep in touch with him. I cared for the sows during farrowing, gave the livestock shots, and delivered several calves. The farming and veterinary skills I'd learned from my granddad were put to good use. In the spring and fall, Joe Barnett and Dr. Calvin Blessing, along with some young men from the BJU dairy farm, came to help me vaccinate and tag the cows.

We wasted nothing. I had long been known as a "scrounger for God." Using bed railings and other scrap metals we accumulated, we built a metal mobile chute and a head gate in our metal shop to work cattle. We built a pig parlor with three farrowing crates where piglets were born, three nursery crates, and three finishing floors. We had a "honey wagon" to draw the hog waste out of the pit below the parlor and put it on the fields. We put a heater in the birthing room for winter deliveries. We raised corn and silage for our animals and had good pasture land. One of my friends told me that if he died and went to Heaven and had to come back as a cow, he wanted to be in the Mission pasture. Of course he was joking, but our neighbors knew we cared for our animals properly.

The farm became an important resource for the Mission—not just a source of income. It provided the therapeutic value of a farm setting for men who were trying to redeem their broken lives. The miracle of life evidenced in every new animal's birth became a topic of discussion for the men. The new crops springing from the ground and the eventual fruits of the harvest gave them hope for their future. We had hoped the men could live on the farm for an extended period of time as they recovered, but the zoning laws prevented that from happening. Sadly, we would never be able to fulfill our vision for a rehabilitation ministry on the farm in Davie County.

After much prayer to discern God's direction for the farm ministry, I once more followed the instruction of Psalm 27:14 and waited on the Lord.

17

GROWING MEN IN CHRIST

Between 1977 and 1987 we experienced remarkable growth in the ministry. God chose that time to reveal the pressing need for me to focus on the fruit we were cultivating at the Mission and complete the renovation of the building that housed it. Therefore, we devoted the next ten years to developing ways to disciple our converts and help them grow in their new found faith. Because of God's wonderful blessing of extra income from the farm, the store, and our newspaper recycling program, we hired more staff to supervise and teach the increasing number of men who came to us.

Bible Course graduates

Through prayer, I sought God's wisdom to guide my decisions concerning the additional programs. People with addictions need ongoing support and encouragement. Our Overcomers program provided an opportunity for "group therapy" through which the men learned to share their problems and work together toward solutions. Mission Fellowship offered a Bible study for the Mission converts to become grounded in God's Word.

We incorporated more prayer opportunities into the life of the Mission. Before the evening services, the saved men attended a prayer meeting where they prayed for the service and the preacher. Each of our departments — store, warehouse, kitchen, Senior Foster Care Division, and cleanup crew — conducted a weekly devotion and shared prayer requests and blessings. The store even put out a prayer box to receive prayer requests from our customers so those requests could be included.

Rev. John D. Moxley, teaching about the Tabernacle

On Veterans Day, we conducted special services to honor the service of the veterans who were staying with us. During the service, some became encouragers giving testimonies of how God spared them and changed their lives. Local churches transported the men to their services and often invited our Mission Trio to sing. For men who desired to know more about God's plan for His people, we provided a Bible correspondence course through which they earned a certificate of accomplishment in Bible study. We even paid tuition for some men to attend night school at Piedmont Bible College.

During this time, God blessed our work in service to Him. Through our programs, we saw some men grow spiritually and take leadership roles in the Mission. Others obtained employment outside the Mission and became active in their churches. While some men recovered their lives because of their time spent at the Mission, not all accepted Christ. But, as we reached more men with God's message of hope and salvation, a significant number of them did accept Jesus Christ as their Lord and Savior. Some of their testimonies are recounted in the part of this book titled Trophies of God's Grace.

Rev. Bill Fryar (left) and Rev. Neal Wilcox in the warehouse

Our service to the needy in the community grew as we expanded our capability to turn donated items into useful furnishings and goods. A welder who came to the Mission built a rack we used to roll mattresses into a sterilizer, one of only sixteen in the state. With it, we sanitized donated mattresses for use at the Mission, or provided them to the needy at low cost or no cost. Someone told us of an elderly lady whose innerspring mattress was so worn that the rusted springs poked her as she lay on it. Our sterilizer enabled us to give her a sanitary, comfortable replacement for it. Deuteronomy 15:11 tells us, "...Thou shalt open thine hand wide unto thy brother, to thy poor, and to thy needy, in thy land." When the warehouse across the street from the Mission became available to us, we were blessed with 40,000 square feet of space that revolutionized our industrial work and housed a store, garage, and adequate space to separate, repair, and restore donations.

In addition to completing the renovations of the Mission building, in 1991, we purchased and renovated the building adjacent to it. We moved five administrative staff offices out of the Mission, which freed that space to accommodate the new programs we implemented. We also constructed a mailroom and a boardroom in which we conducted staff meetings and hosted luncheons for the Mission Board. These areas were also used by our volunteers to prepare our donor newsletter for mailing and to package complete Thanksgiving and Christmas meals for distribution to hundreds of needy families identified by the local churches.

Volunteers preparing mailings

This was a time when the Mission received significant exposure in local newspapers. Through articles written about our activities, events, and human interest stories, people learned more about our ministry and how God was working through it. Realizing that something special was at work in the Mission, people became more supportive through donations of resources and time, and many remembered the Mission with their bequests. People, who ten years previously had viewed the Mission as little more than a place with a bed and a meal for derelicts, now welcomed it as a contributing member of the neighborhood that received the indigent and returned productive men back to the community.

As a self-styled "investigative reporter," Billy Joe Kepley had visited and participated in several charitable organizations, such as the Salvation Army Soup Line, to "get the scoop" on how they operated and write articles about his experiences. He came to the Mission to interview me about the history and operation of our Mission. I talked with him at length regarding the various Mission activities, the rules and expectations we had for our clients, and I gave him a tour of all our facilities except the farm. But, as I later learned, this was only the first part of Kepley's research. Along with two friends, Kepley showed up at the Mission one night disguised as transient street people. He wanted to find out how he would be treated if he came to us as an indigent. He and his friends were treated like all our men — with kindness and love. That night he heard stories from men who told him that the first chance they ever got in life was when they came to the Mission. He learned that my answers during our interview were not just words, but a commitment to the ministry of reclamation of forgotten souls demonstrated with action.

Human interest articles in the *Winston-Salem Journal* featured two men whose families were well-known at that time. Woo Eng Bunker was the grandson of Eng Bunker, one of the original Siamese twins, Eng and Chang, who traveled with the Barnum and Bailey Circus in the early 1900s. Since Woo E. was seventy-four years old when he arrived, he stayed in our Senior Foster Care Division. Charles Edward Mabry came to the Mission at the age of sixty-seven, after a bout with the bottle. Charles' uncle, Ed Mabry, owned one of the most photographed places in the United States—Mabry Mill on the Blue Ridge Parkway in Patrick County, Virginia. Both of these men gave the reporter a nostalgic look into their past lives and insight into their lives at the Mission.

As we developed programs that grew the Mission ministry, I continued to pray for the time and the location for expanding the farm ministry. The vision of a place in the country where men could recover and rehabilitate remained on my heart. In Matthew 21:22 Christ tells us, "And all things, whatsoever ye shall ask in prayer, believing, ye shall receive." I knew that if my dream for this program was to be achieved, it would be through God's power, not mine.

18

A MILESTONE CELEBRATION

I n 1992, we celebrated the Mission's twenty-fifth anniversary with a banquet in the Piedmont Bible College
gymnasium. Several dignitaries from the Winston-Salem
city government attended, including Mayor Martha Wood,
who proclaimed September 14-21, 1992, Winston-Salem
Rescue Mission week. Members of the Mission Board,
Mission friends, former Mission staff members, pastors,
missionaries, friends and family honored our service at this
occasion.

Board of Directors

Barbara and I received many tokens of appreciation for our years of service to the homeless, including letters from the Honorable Jim Martin, governor of North Carolina; Senator Jesse Helms; and President George W. Bush. On behalf of the Mission Board of Directors, Stuart Epperson, the first president of the board, presented us with a beautiful plaque commemorating our twenty-five years of service.

More than fifty pastors and missionaries attended the banquet, several of whom had been our friends and colleagues for years. Rev. Don Horton, a pastor from Statesville, North Carolina, came. Rev. Horton was a past president of the board and had held services at the Mission on the fourth Saturday night of the month throughout those twenty-five years. Former staff members in attendance included Rev. Ernie Mills and Rev. Bill Fryar, each of whom had become an Executive Director of Missions. Rev. Mills serves in Durham, North Carolina, and, until he retired in 1995, Rev. Fryar served in Florence, South Carolina. My mentor in the ministry of rescue, Rev. Wayman Pritchard, Executive Director of the Raleigh Rescue Mission, Raleigh, North Carolina, and his wife Dot also attended. Rev. Kaleel Ellison, Executive Director of the City Rescue Mission of Jacksonville, Florida, and president of the IUGM (International Union of Gospel Missions) was there with his talented wife Jackie, who provided the special music for our anniversary celebration. Because I had been elected president of the South-Eastern District of the IUGM, I was privileged to serve on its board for four years. IUGM changed its name to AGRM (Association of Gospel Rescue Missions) in 2000. The AGRM is comprised of more than 450 rescue mission workers from all over the world. Rev. Ellison presented me with the president's award for twenty-five years of faithful service to the homeless.

Following the festivities, we conducted an offertory service and were blessed with a significant donation that helped with the cost of resurfacing the exterior of the Mission building. But the gift we still treasure the most is the gift from our daughter.

Beverly and her husband of two years, Dan Beadles, attended the anniversary celebration. Bev met Dan, a young man from Pekin, Illinois, while they were both attending BJU. During their senior year, Dan asked me for Bev's hand in marriage. They were married on August 18, 1990. We are very thankful that our daughter and son-in-law are faithful to the Lord. They have raised our grandchildren to serve the Lord and be active in our current church, Morningside Baptist Church, Greenville, South Carolina.

Ryan, Dan, Beverly, and Caroline Beadles

Without Barbara and my knowing, Bev had asked Brother Joe Bowman, President of the Mission Board, for an opportunity to say a few words. Through the eyes of a child raised in the environment of a rescue mission, she so eloquently expressed the challenges, blessings, and joys of rescue ministry. When Bev took the podium she read a letter she had prepared for us that I now share with you:

September 14, 1992

Dear Dad and Mom,

I can't believe it has been 25 years, can you? I've only been around for 24 of those years, but many times you have explained to me how the Lord led you to Winston from Greenville. Did you think He would leave you here that long?

Tonight is a time to look back at the good times, and some not-so-good times. I'd like to take just a minute to share with you and our friends here a few of our memories.

There was one night I remember just vaguely. We received a phone call there was a fire on Trade St. We rushed downtown to find the banana warehouse was burning. The old mission building windows were scorched, but it was spared.

How about the night, Dad, you and I went out at about 9:00 to try to get some cows back in the pasture? But that was no average night— it was Halloween, and I had visions of us, or the cows, getting egged by some prankster. Thankfully we got the cows back safely.

The good memories abound too. Maybe not so many big ones as lots of little ones. For one thing, it was always neat to think I was the only kid in town to grow up in a rescue mission. And I always felt safe there because I always had a friend close by.

Even at age 5 or 6, I felt like a part of the mission. There was always some job to do—real important things to do like rolling pennies and stuffing the newsletters. I remember my "office" where I "x"ed all those 3x5 cards.

Another of my memories is visiting different churches every Sunday and Wednesday night. We would often go over to the pastor's house for snacks and fellowship. And oh the stories they could tell...I could listen for hours.

Anniversaries were special nights, too, and I particularly enjoyed hearing Clebe McClary speak of overcoming personal tragedy and Dr. Al Smith give the history of the song and then sing it. We would always go out to eat with the speaker before the service — that was a big highlight for me, the speakers were always good. But, if I had to pick a favorite it would be Mr. John Horan. I wish I could remember more of his stories of being in the mafia before getting saved and eventually directing a mission in Florida. No doubt he is looking down from heaven with a big smile on his face. It will be good to see him again one day.

Mom and Dad, the ministry you have had to the homeless in Winston for 25 years has been blessed greatly by the Lord. We have seen souls saved, lives changed and homes put back together. The Lord has blessed with facilities beyond what was ever dreamed. It is exciting to look ahead and wonder how else He will choose to use and bless you.

AND TONIGHT WE'D LIKE TO TELL YOU
OF A BLESSING TO BE
FOR OUR LITTLE HOUSEHOLD WILL

SOON INCLUDE THREE
WE KNOW YOU WILL BE EXCITED
AS YOU SHOULD BE
FOR YOU WILL BE GRANDPARENTS
IN 1993.

Along with six hundred friends and guests, we learned our little girl was going to bless us with a grandchild! Many of our friends still remind us of what a special moment this was.

* * *

Since then Dan and Bev have raised two wonderful children who love and serve the Lord. Many times as they were growing up, our precious grandchildren came to the Mission to sing for the men. A favorite song was, "This Little Light of Mine." Like their mother, their sweet presence at the Mission could soften even the most hardened men.

Caroline and Ryan Beadles

19

CAMP ASHBURN ACRES

———————◆———————

Learning of the blessing of a grandchild was the most important personal news Barbara and I received in 1992. We were ecstatic! But God was also working to bless us with the answer to my prayer for expanding the services of our farm ministry.

Over the years, the challenges facing rescue ministries evolved as our society and culture changed. We began to see increasing numbers of young men who had dropped out of college and out of life because their addiction to alcohol, or any number of street drugs, impaired their thinking. These men needed to be retrained and prepared to face the challenges of seeking and holding a job. They needed to be empowered by God's love to resist the temptations of the world and returned to society as productive men ready to raise families and serve the Lord in their communities. This was the vision we had for the future of our farm ministry—a place where lost souls could be saved and men rehabilitated so that they could rebuild their lives.

Brother Haynes Moore served as the Director of Public Relations for the Mission and also helped me manage the Mission. He and I had long been prayer partners concerning the future of this ministry. We were committed to relocating the farm to a place where we could have a long-term ministry to help the younger men who came to us. Rev. Moore lived in Yadkin County and he was familiar with the available properties suitable for achieving our vision. Finally, we located Camp Ashburn Acres. When we contacted the owner, Mr. Ashburn, he told us to contact his realtor for the details concerning the property. The realtor told us the prop-

Rev. Wilcox and Rev. Moore

erty consisted of 110 acres of partly wooded land on which there was some fenced pasture and three lakes. Structures on the property included a lodge, a five-room brick house, a two-car garage, a utility building, and a large recreational building. It sounded ideal for our ministry. Based on the information from the realtor, the Mission Board gave permission for us to proceed with our efforts to acquire the property.

After several weeks of trying, we finally made contact with the realtor, only to find out that Mr. Ashburn had decided not to sell. Instead, he planned to build a house on the property to use as his retirement home. We had visualized the camp as being the perfect place for the new farm. This news was very disappointing. I could not believe the door had closed to the only suitable property we had found. This was an impossible challenge with no earthly way of resolving it. I put my trust in the Lord, realizing I needed to add to those calluses on my knees and pray that He would reveal His will for the farm's future.

Six months passed. As I continued to pray for guidance, the Lord seemed to tell me, "You haven't done your best until you talk to Mr. Ashburn personally." My only question was, "How do I talk to this man?" But, with the Lord telling me that I needed to talk to Mr. Ashburn, I set my mind to determining the best way to approach him about his plans for the property. I studied the matter from all sides, spending many hours praying that God would give me the words to say to Mr. Ashburn. He and his wife attended church, and I knew that, if it was in God's will, He could change their minds about selling the property. I shared my burden with Barbara, and she began to pray with me.

I finally mustered up the courage to call Mr. Ashburn and arranged to meet with him to discuss the property. When we sat down in his living room to talk, I believe my time in prayer encouraged me to step out boldly in faith. I asked Mr. Ashburn if he envisioned his retirement as mowing grass and doing all the work needed to maintain the buildings on the property. Then I asked if he would consider letting someone else do all those chores. If he would, I offered that perhaps we could work out a deal for our mutual benefit. When we concluded our conversation, I gave him my business card. He said he'd call me. I thanked him for his time and drove away, leaving the matter in the Lord's hands.

After a week had passed with no call from Mr. Ashburn, I admit I worried that purchasing Camp Ashburn Acres might not happen. However, I focused on God working His will in the farm ministry. In all my years of service to the Lord, He had never failed me. No matter His answer to me, obedience to His will has always been my response to Him.

At last, the call came. Mr. Ashburn had a proposal concerning his property and suggested we meet. I immediately contacted the Mission Board members and asked them to pray for our meeting. I met with Mr. Ashburn, and he told me his asking price for the property. He said he wanted to live on the property for three years, during which time we could lease the land and move our animals from Davie County onto the property. He would deduct the lease payments from the asking price, and a balloon payment for the remainder would come due at the end of the three years. When I presented this plan to the board, they accepted it.

I look back in amazement at how the Lord seemed to be directing this vision. "Be still and know that I *am* God...." (Ps. 46:10) Trusting the Lord, waiting on His timing, and allowing Him to work through a situation can sometimes be difficult, but when you do, the results are often nothing less than miraculous. So it was for us with the farm ministry. God gave us the opportunity and the challenge to develop the ministry we envisioned. During the three years Mr. Ashburn had requested, 1993 to 1996, we organized the farm, developed a rehabilitation program, searched for staff, and planned the housing for the staff and for the men we would help. Those three years also gave us a reasonable amount of time to raise the money to pay for the property.

If we were to accomplish what the Lord had set before us, there was still much to do, and do it we would—a day at a time, as the Lord led and provided.

20

A PLACE OF NEW BEGINNINGS

Our new ministry needed a name. Choosing a name that reflected the mission of the ministry was important. Our new farm would become a place where troubled young men could retreat to a quiet rural setting where they could learn to have a personal relationship with God. And that relationship would translate into their everyday lives, leading them to Christ-like living. Mrs. Lois Bowman, who worked in the office at the Mission, suggested Alpha Acres, "a place of new beginnings." That was exactly what this ministry would be for those who came to us—a new beginning!

On April 13, 1993, our family received the blessing of a new beginning. We welcomed our grandson Ryan Sterling Beadles into the family. Beverly and Dan lived in Greenville, South Carolina, about three hours away. Barbara and I left for Greenville soon after Dan had called to let us know the baby was coming. Ryan was born shortly after we arrived. God is so good! As I looked at Ryan, the memories of my grandfather flooded into my mind. I prayed that Ryan and I would have the same special relationship I had shared with my grandfather.

It would be three years to the day during a visit with Bev's family to celebrate Ryan's third birthday that he would excitedly announce his good news to Barbara and me, "I'm going to be a big brother!" On September 24, 1996, our family was blessed with Ryan's little sister, Caroline Joy Beadles.

Upon returning to Winston-Salem, I turned my attention to staffing Alpha Acres. As I reviewed the IUGM's list of prospective employees, one couple stood out, Rev. Richard and Mrs. Angie Lockhart from West Virginia. They were seeking a place where they could serve the Lord together. Rev. Lockhart had ten years of experience in rescue mission ministry and had served for several years as the Executive Director of a small mission in Tennessee. I contacted the Lockharts and invited them to visit Alpha Acres. Upon arrival, they crossed the yard near the lodge and looked across the lake. Mrs. Lockhart was so overcome by the beauty of the setting that she began to weep. She later said, "As we walked the property, we saw the possibilities for serving God in a ministry in such a beautiful place." The Lockharts were ready and waiting.

I recognized the Lockharts' strong desire to develop and implement the program we had envisioned and prayed for at Alpha Acres. So, in June 1997, the Lockharts moved to Yadkin County. In August, they opened Alpha Acres.

Richard and Angie Lockhart

We sent Rev. Lockhart and two others, Rev. Gene McDuffy and Mr. Lynn Holloway, to the Los Angeles Rescue Mission in California, for training in a program being used by that mission to educate their clients. The program, which was similar to the Accelerated Christian Education used by Christian church schools, allowed each pupil to learn at his own pace and was tailored specifically to the needs of the homeless population. After we renovated the lodge and created a learning center, a friend was led by the Lord to donate the remainder of the funds we needed to buy twelve computers to start the educational program. The implementation of this program at Alpha Acres enabled students to attain their GED (General Educational Development) diplomas, and some even went on to complete college.

A young man named Mark came to Alpha Acres in the fall of 1997. He was illiterate and struggling with addiction. At the age of thirty, while living at Alpha Acres, Mark learned to read, and he invited the Lord into his heart. Through reading, Mark met his Savior in the pages of the Bible and understood the importance of knowing Him personally. Mrs. Lockhart helped Mark to read The Christmas

Story from Matthew 1:18-25 for the first time. We were so excited for him. With our encouragement, this young man who once asked me "Can you imagine seeing a sign and not knowing what it says?" was given the opportunity to read The Christmas Story on the Channel 8 television station in High Point, North Carolina.

Mrs. Lockhart managed the kitchen and supervised the men who worked there. She planned the menus, ordered the food, and usually assigned one of the men to be the cook. The downtown Mission shared food that was donated to us with Alpha Acres. Twice a week I delivered the food to Alpha Acres and met with the staff to discuss the progress of our clients. A grocery store in Yadkinville, a small town nearby, donated some food—mostly pastries and bread. We were grateful for everything we received from the grocery store. But, on one occasion, the men had asked Mrs. Lockhart if they could have bacon, and on another, they requested corn dogs. Mrs. Lockhart prayed for both of these requests, and God moved the heart of the store manager to provide both items. While God provided greatly for the needs of the ministry, we were reminded that He never overlooks even the smallest request asked by a faithful servant in His name. Jesus tells us, "If ye shall ask any thing in my name, I will do *it*." (John 14:14)

Every Sunday and Wednesday night, Rev. Haynes Moore and I visited churches to promote the downtown Mission and Alpha Acres. Rev. Lockhart brought men from Alpha Acres to churches in Yadkin County. We sent representatives to all pastors' fellowship meetings in the area. Our presence in the churches increased awareness of Alpha Acres, which increased support for it.

God had laid the vision for Alpha Acres on my heart when I recognized the "revolving door" attitude of some of the young men at the Mission. They would come in, get sober, and in a few days were back on the streets pursuing the same addictions that had brought them to the Mission in the first place. I knew we needed more time with them to "dry" them out and get them thinking clearly so the Holy Spirit could begin to work in their lives. Alpha Acres gave us the time we needed to disciple them, educate them, and teach them job skills. Our ninety-day program eventually expanded to twelve months.

To this day, Alpha Acres continues its ministry to rescue men in body and spirit, and glorify God by returning the homeless, addicted, and needy as fully participating members of society contributing their skills and experiences to their communities. As God's servants in this ministry, we believe the transforming power of Jesus Christ makes a difference in men's lives. We believe evangelism through Bible study, church attendance, and Bible-based counseling generates new and wholesome attitudes toward life. We believe education, coupled with work assignments, adds structure to unstructured lives while developing job-skills training that increase the person's value as an employee. To complete the process of growing toward wholeness in Christ, and from poverty to economic and emotional independence, men need to depend on God and have marketable skills. Graduates of Alpha Acres participate in a graduation ceremony, complete with cap and gown, and receive a certificate of accomplishment. But, more importantly, they receive the life-changing lessons from the Word of God that will never fail them.

I would like to share the salvation stories of two of these young men who, by the grace of God, were saved and turned their lives around at Alpha Acres.

* * *

Paul Furrow came to Alpha Acres in 2001. Paul was raised in a loving Christian home. One summer, while attending a vacation Bible study, he came to understand that he was a sinner and asked Jesus into his life and was saved.

Paul says, "My life was peaceful and at times I was on fire for the Lord and everything was fine. But, as time went on, I allowed myself to succumb to peer-pressure and started experimenting with alcohol and drugs. As time passed, it became easier to put the things of the Lord behind me and

Paul Furrow

to go out to seek worldly pleasures. Then, after a perceived insult, I turned my back on the church completely. Over the course of the next few years I experimented in all kinds of fleshly activities, trying to fill in the hole that seemed to be inside me."

Paul was to find that no amount of alcohol, drugs, or immorality was going to satisfy his need. He knew there was a better way to live. In desperation, he was contemplating suicide after he lost his wife, job, money, and home.

Paul says, "During the night of August 11, 2001, when I was at my lowest, God spoke in the small part of my heart and let me know it wasn't my life, but His, and that He was not finished with me yet. I came back to the Lord on August 12, and that was when I was directed to a place called Alpha Acres." Although at first apprehensive, Paul continues, "It was a life-altering experience. Dr. Lockhart and Brother Agee were wonderfully patient men who answered my questions and gave me a new thirst for knowledge. It was a true blessing to be able to slow down and listen to the Lord and to have the opportunity to visit various churches and hear many different styles of preaching. Plus, the classroom teaching was invaluable. After graduating from the program, I have continued to attend church services at one of the churches that help support the ministry, and the Lord even blessed me to be a musician in the choir."

Paul's father passed away in 2003. Paul says, "I can't imagine having come through that without God's grace." Paul has been employed at River Burch Lodge since it opened in 2005. He says, "It truly was the Lord's plan for me when he sent me to Alpha Acres, because it gave me the time to become the adult I was supposed to be. I praise the Lord for the vision He gave Brother Wilcox and for all the wonderful staff at the farm and at the Rescue Mission."

* * *

Growing up, Luke Money did not have a strong Christian family influence in his life. The peer groups he hung out with soon led him to a life of drugs and alcohol. He felt his life slipping out of control with no hope in sight. His wife was ready to leave and take their newborn baby because of his addiction. He says, "I could not go any farther; all had failed."

After completing two secular rehab treatment programs, his parents made arrangements for him to come to Alpha Acres. Luke says, "It truly was a new beginning in my life. The staff taught me straight from the Bible how to resist temptation and start a new life with Christ. The Lord saved me in August 2004. My life has been different every since the day I asked Jesus to be Lord of my life. The Lord restored my marriage, and I am so glad I have my wife and sons, instead of being in prison or dead."

In November 2004, the Lord called Luke to preach. After finishing the Alpha Acres program, he attended Piedmont Baptist College. It took Luke more than six years to complete his education. When his first son, Brock, was born, Luke was strung out on drugs. He was with his wife Holly when their second son Carter was born. Even though he had to work two and three jobs to support his family while going through

Luke Money and Family

college, he made time for those he loved. While in college, Luke was active in Peace Haven Baptist Church, the church he attended while at Alpha Acres. He directed the children's church program and was also on the board of New Hope Pregnancy Care in Yadkinville. He preached several times at revivals in the area. In May 2012, Luke graduated from Calvary Bible College, founded by Rev. Roger Baker, a former staff member of the Rescue Mission and, for many years, the pastor of Calvary Baptist Church in King, North Carolina. This was the difference Christ made in Luke's life.

God continued to work in Luke's life as he served at Alpha Acres on the weekends. In April of 2011, he became the Chaplin at Alpha Acres. Then, in January 2012, Luke was asked to be the manager of the ministry where the Lord first made the difference in his life. Now, in turn, he is helping make a difference in the lives of others who are hurting.

* * *

One of the greatest thrills in the ministry of rescue is to see your vision come to fruition and have no explanation to offer except, "Our God did another miracle." There are many testimonies of salvation and changed lives from men who have passed through Alpha Acres, more than can be recounted here, and, as the work at Alpha Acres continues, assuredly there will be many more. "Being confident of this very thing, that he which hath begun a good work in you will perform it until the day of Jesus Christ:" (Phil. 1:6)

21

THE WORK OF GOD'S MISSION CONTINUES

…. For what is your life? It is even a vapor, that appeareth for a little time, and then vanisheth away. Jas. 4:14

The years between 1967 and 1998 had been filled with opportunities to further God's kingdom work. We had accomplished so much through His grace, provision, and leading. But, in 1998, my by-pass surgery made me realize that I was no longer the young man of thirty-one years ago who had so eagerly accepted the call to serve full-time in rescue ministry. Barbara and I believed God was telling us it was time for a younger couple to continue His work in Winston-Salem. The Board and I prayed for two years to prepare for my impending retirement.

Dan Parsons became the new Executive Director of the Mission. Brother Parsons, a leader in his church with years of business experience with the J.G. Messick Company, had served several terms on the Rescue Mission Board. Brother Parsons was a hometown man and very familiar with the area. He worked beside me for more than a year until I retired in September 2000. We had a wonderful service and retirement reception at Union Grove Baptist Church, pastored by Dr. Harold Fletcher. While Barbara continued to assist Brother Parsons' wife, Anne, in the office until 2003, after thirty-three years as the Executive Director of the Winston-Salem Rescue Mission, it was time for me to pass the baton.

Dan and Anne Parsons with Neal and Barbara Wilcox

My prayer was that Brother Parsons would take the Rescue Mission to the next level of service for the Lord in Winston-Salem. There was still much to be done and plenty of homeless and needy families waiting to be served and saved. While I could no longer serve in full-time rescue ministry, I prayed the Lord would provide opportunities for me to continue in His service — He did.

I have been privileged to help several missions through their transition period when their director was being replaced. I helped the Piedmont Rescue Mission in Burlington, North Carolina; The Good Samaritan Ministry in Jackson Hole, Wyoming; and the Union Mission of Roanoke Rapids, North Carolina. Barbara and I moved to Greenville, South Carolina, in 2007 to be close to our daughter and her family.

Until his retirement in December 2013, Brother Parsons continued to expand the work of the Rescue Mission. He launched a major building program and dedicated a beautiful new four-story New Life Center in 2008. The New Life Center increased the services and the number of people served at the Mission. The former Administration Building was converted to house the medical and dental community outreach services offered. I was truly humbled when it was renamed The Neal Wilcox Center in 2008.

The part of this book titled Trophies of God's Grace contains only a few testimonies of men who found salvation and a new beginning at the Winston-Salem Rescue Mission and Alpha Acres. Since my retirement, many more have come to know the Lord through the continuing service of Brother Parsons and his staff.

Your continued prayer and support for this ministry is greatly appreciated by the staff as they reach out to the hurting in Winston-Salem.

TROPHIES OF GOD'S GRACE

---◆---

3For I rejoiced greatly, when the brethren came and testified of the truth that is in thee, even as thou walkest in truth.

4I have no greater joy than to hear that my children walk in truth.

3 John 1:3-4

Through the work done in His name at the Winston-Salem Rescue Mission, God worked miracles in the lives of the men whose testimonies are presented here, as written. To the best of my knowledge, the year in which they gave their testimonies of salvation is accurate. Their stories are representative of so many more who passed through our doors and found new life in Christ. Not only were their lives profoundly changed, but their families were also touched by God's redemptive power. Following these testimonies is just a sampling of the many letters of appreciation received by the Rescue Mission from family members, as well as from other supportive friends of the Mission.

1967

Audley Blaine Fox was born in August of 1916. Blaine, as we knew him, faced many challenges as he grew up. His mother left him with friends when he was six years old and he never saw her again. His dad died when Blaine was eight. As a child, he worked on a relative's farm for room and board. He had an eighth grade education. Later, Blaine spent four years in the army serving his country in World War II. At one time, he worked for Ford Motor Company, and then he worked wherever he could to support his wife and four children. In September 1966, his wife Gladys died suddenly from a heart attack, leaving him alone to care for their children. Four days later, drunk, discouraged, and at his wits end Audley sat next to the same couch on which Gladys had died. Then, because of his drinking, he had to deal

Audley Blaine Fox

with the loss of his children. Drinking became his only escape from a life of loss and failure;

In September of 1967, Blaine lost custody of his children to the foster care system in North Carolina. That was the last straw; now he had nothing to come home to but the empty house and his bottle. Neither one did much to lift his spirits or give him a life he cared to live. In the latter part of 1967, Blaine found his way to the Winston-Salem Rescue Mission where he was welcomed and given food, a bed, and was shown the love of God from the Bible, the staff, and the men at the Mission. Soon he understood his need for Christ as his personal Savior and asked Him into his heart.

Blaine met and became good friends with Joseph Sauter, who had also recently trusted Christ at the Mission. Joe was a carpenter and drywall finisher. The two men bonded and became good friend for the rest of their lives. Together they renovated the left side of the basement in the Mission. They were the first to receive beds in the renovated area.

Blaine needed to get a job and make plans to get his children back. A Christian couple, Archie and Grace Cook, owned and operated Archie's Lunch, which was located a few blocks from the Mission. They hired Blaine to be a busboy and dishwasher. They took him to church with them. This kind couple learned about his desire to provide for his children and helped him work toward his goal to get them back.

Joe did not have a problem getting a job and soon Joe and Blaine were working outside the Mission, but they were still happy to do what they could to help the Mission. Within a few months, they each rented their own apartment in the same building and moved out of the Mission.

By Easter 1968, Blaine got visitation rights to have all his children home for the holiday. The two oldest stayed with their dad, who was sober and working regularly for the first time in over a year. At last, Blaine felt good about what was happening in his life, now that he had trusted the Lord and was trying to live for Him. He soon also got his two younger children back. The Cooks stood by Blaine and his children. They did not have children of their own, and it was as if they adopted Blaine's children.

Blaine's friend Joe met a young lady and they were soon married. He and his wife helped Debbie, Blaine's daughter, to get her GED so she could go to college. In the early 1970s,

Joe developed leukemia and only lived a short time leaving Donna, his wife, and their little boy. Debbie said, "Joe was always kind and caring for her and her siblings."

Blaine worked and took care of his children and made sure they were in church. Debbie told me that her dad always loved the Rescue Mission and reminded his children that, if they supported a charity, remember the Mission, where people help to mend lives and put families back together.

Audley Blaine Fox passed away in November 1983 lying on his bed, giving gratitude to his Lord for forgiveness and salvation. On his last day, he told Debbie that his place was prepared and he was ready to go where it was always light and there was no night. God made a way for Blaine to raise his children before he took him home. After Blaine put his trust in Christ, God seemed to put people in his life to help and encourage him along the way.

When we want to do right, God and His children will help us.

1968

Tex Ashley was born in Wilkes County and raised in a family of nine children. Tex's family moved to Elkin, North Carolina, when Tex was twelve-years old. At the age of sixteen, he helped his dad serve bootleg liquor to the customers who came to their home. Unfortunately, Tex had a habit of sampling every jug before serving the guests. This led to a craving for alcohol that caused him to spend many years of his life in prison and on the chain gang. He was a mechanic on the outside, but in prison he was a cook.

Tex first came to the Mission in 1968, after his family broke up and he had been on a drinking spree. He frequently came to us over the next twelve years. In 1981, while Tex was staying at the Mission, an officer from Elkin arrested him on an old warrant. I told the officer how well Tex was doing this time and that we would be glad to take him back. While waiting in jail for his trial, a visiting minister came to Tex's cell and led Tex to the Lord. Based on the recommendation of the arresting officer, the judge had mercy on Tex and allowed him to come back to us. Several weeks later, Tex's mom called to tell me of how excited she and his dad were about the change in their son's life, in answer to their prayers. Tex got a job, paid his fine, and started attending church with his boss. Tex soon moved out of the Mission to live on his own. In 1984, Tex came back to the Mission, rededicated his life to the Lord, and started working for the Mission. He repaired donated cars and trucks and kept our fleet of vehicles up and running. By this time, we had our own garage inside of our warehouse, and he could service our vehicles on the premises.

Tex Ashley

There were times when Tex worked extremely hard to keep our trucks running so that we could make our pickups and keep our customers happy. I remember a time in the early 1970s, before he was convicted on a DUI

(driving under the influence); Tex made one hundred donations pickups in one day. That was a record that, as of this
writing, has never been broken.

After having his license revoked and advised that he
could never get them back, he asked me to help him apply
for them. Tex had been sober four years, the longest period
of time since he was a teenager serving alcohol to his dad's
customers. I went with him to appear before a judge and
explained the change in Tex's life and that he had been at
the Mission four years. The Lord answered our prayers,
and his license was reinstated. Tex never drank again.

Tex often visited his mom in Elkin on the weekends.
Since his dad had passed away, his mom enjoyed having
someone to go to church with her. After his mom died,
Tex eventually moved back to Elkin and drove to Winston-
Salem every day to faithfully serve the Lord at the Mission.
Tex, like so many others, wanted to thank the Lord and the
Mission for being there for him all those years when he
was not serving the Lord. He dearly loved the Mission for
what it meant to him before he trusted the Lord—but even
more afterwards. He would do anything for the Mission
and the staff.

In 2000, Tex began to have shortness of breath caused by
emphysema. If he exerted himself very much, he had to sit
down and catch his breath. One morning when he did not
come to the Mission, we became concerned. We soon found
out that he had been taken to the hospital with breathing
problems. While at the hospital Tex had a heart attack and
died. His brother, Jimmy, took the responsibility for the
funeral arrangements. I, along with Rev. Haynes Moore,
the Director of Public Relations for the Rescue Mission, was
asked to have part in his funeral.

On February 27, 2001, my dear friend was buried in
East Elkin Full Gospel Church cemetery. While writing this
book, I talked with Jimmy about Tex's passing. Jimmy told

me how he too had dedicated his life to the Lord now and was looking forward to seeing Tex, along with his mom and dad, in Heaven.

The Mission is the place where the Lord answered the prayers of many moms, dads and siblings regarding the Spiritual needs of their loved ones. Thanks be to the Lord!

1969

Jim Belton spent ten years in the Marine Corps where he had attained the rank of Sergeant. In 1965, Jim was riding with a friend who was driving under the influence. When the automobile crashed, Jim was thrown through the windshield. He landed on a tree stump and broke his back, ruptured his spleen, and destroyed a kidney. Jim was in the hospital for eight months in a cast from his ankle to his neck. He was told he would never walk again and would be permanently disabled if he lived.

Bradford (Bunk) Sparks, Jim's uncle, took him to his home where Bunk's family nursed Jim back to health. Bunk eventually built a small block house close to his home to give Jim some privacy. Not being able to work and getting a disability check, Jim was left with a lot of time for mischief. Jim began to drink more and more. Finally, Jim lost his driver's license after a DUI conviction. Things only got worse from that point on.

In 1969, Bunk talked Jim into coming to the Rescue Mission. It was here where Jim trusted Christ as his Savior and dedicated himself to the Lord and to the Mission. He became our kitchen manager and cook, when needed. But Jim was more than that; he was very dependable in taking on responsibility around the Mission. I never thought of Jim as being disabled. He seemed to love to help the Mission. He was like family. My daughter enjoyed going to the Mission with me to see Jimmie, as she called him. He always gave her candy and presents. When I spoke in local churches, Jim enjoyed going with me to give his testimony.

Jim was always looking for ways he could help the Mission. He repaired lawnmowers by using parts from one old mower to repair another. He designed and built the table saw we used to cut up the scrap lumber we gave to needy families.

I helped Jim get his driver's license back. He soon bought a car and was able to visit his family. A young lady

living near the Mission caught Jim's eye. She was not a church-going person. She and Jim eventually got married, and Jim moved out of the Mission. In a few months the marriage ended, so Jim went back to his family. He had a sister in Charlotte and a brother in Summerfield, North Carolina, both of whom welcomed him into their homes. He visited the Mission occasionally. I was always glad to see him, and he seemed glad to see us.

Jim Belton

Many years later I received phone call from Philip, Jim's brother, telling me of Jim's death and asking me to officiate his funeral. Jim was not just one of the men; he was special. Following the funeral, Barbara reminded me that, after he returned home, the Mission received a check from Jim every month.

I thank Jim's family and friends who supported the Mission in appreciation for what it did for him. I am reminded there are many Jim Beltons out there in the world today without hope and needing help. They need the Lord as Jim did and by his grace they could be a wonderful uncle, brother, and yes, grandson, son, or dad. Ask the Lord what He would have you do to reach the homeless and hurting in your neighborhood. Not everyone who comes to the Mission is willing to accept salvation, but Bunk's nephew did.

* * *

Robert Luck first came to the Mission in 1969 after losing his driver's license as a result of driving under the influence. When he arrived, he was waiting for his court appearance and planned to stay at the Mission only until he got the verdict. This turned out to be the first of many stays at the Mission. Robert felt cared for at the Mission. It was a place that reminded him of his spiritual needs while caring for his physical needs. But you might say that he was using the Mission when he needed it and was not really interested in a permanent change in his life.

Robert was born into a loving family of seven children in May 1936. Robert started drinking at the age of sixteen. He was known to be a quiet man, even when he was under the influence of alcohol. Robert tried to work and support his wife and his daughter, Wanda. He would work for a period of time, but eventually his drinking would cost him his job. This went on for many years. Unfortunately, differences between Robert and his first wife led to their divorce in 1974. Robert stayed in touch with Wanda and tried to be there for her as much as his life-style could afford. Over the years, whenever he came to the Mission, I often asked him about Wanda.

Even though he had a problem with alcohol, Robert was not a bum. He was sober during the many times he stayed with us, and he worked and carried his load. He knew if he didn't remain sober at the Mission, he would lose his place to sleep. He also knew that, if he wanted to get a job outside the Mission, he could stay with us until he found his own accommodations.

Robert and Glenda Luck

In 1994, Billy Joe Willard, Robert's lifelong friend, introduced Robert to Glenda Jordan. Three months later Robert was hurt very deeply when Billy Joe died from bone cancer. But Robert and Glenda began dating and soon were married. They visited Union Grove Baptist Church. Dr. Harold Fletcher, one of the founders and a board member of the Rescue Mission, was the pastor there. Although Robert had made a profession of faith when he was thirteen years old, he had strayed away from the Lord. After more than twenty years of wandering his own path, Robert finally went forward and confessed his sins for the years he was away from the Lord and asked the Lord to forgive him. Robert has said that the years since his return to Christ have been the best years of his life. Both Robert and Glenda attend church regularly; Glenda sings in the choir.

Neither Robert nor I knew that through all those years Robert had been checking in and out of the Mission and struggling with his addiction, two of his sisters and a niece were helping to support the Mission financially and praying that he would not only get physical help but also spiritual help.

Robert nearly died several times in the emergency room from a heart problem. He thanks the Lord that with the help of two pacemakers and a defibrillator he is still with us. Robert has said, "I thank the Lord for the Mission being there for me when I needed it and helping me through the problem years of my life. I thank God for sparing me through all my troubles and difficulties and giving my wife and me these good years together. Thank the Lord for those who never quit praying for a miracle in the ministry of rescue." Robert told me he always appreciated what the Mission staff did for him during the many times he came through our doors.

In 2012, my wife and I were visiting the Baptist Hospital in Winston-Salem. As I entered an admissions office I heard a lady call my name. She asked me if I remembered Robert Luck. I said, "Of course I do." She told me she was his niece. She told me about his marriage to Glenda and that he attended church regularly and was doing well. She gave me his phone number so I could get this testimony.

* * *

Blaine Gray, or "Pop" as we respectfully called him, came to the Rescue Mission in the summer of 1969 — homeless, hungry and needing a friend. The Mission was able to meet his physical needs and, after attending services for several months, Pop accepted Christ as his Savior and became our dishwasher. At seventy years old, even with glasses, his vision was not good, but he was willing to give the stubborn egg-stained dishes a second and third washing to get them clean.

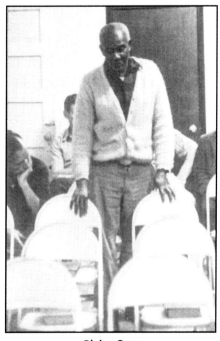

Blaine Gray

I asked Pop to go with me to the Cherry Street Correctional Center and tell the men there what Christ had done for him. You see, Pop had been on and off the chain gang for many years. These men had known Blaine as one of their peers. It was exciting to hear him tell the prisoners about what Christ had done for him. Pop stayed with us until his health forced him to go to a rest home. He faithfully served his Lord. Sometime later I attended his funeral.

1970

Henry B. Hinson hitchhiked into Winston-Salem on September 9, 1970. Tired and weary from being on the road all day and sleeping on the ground at night, he was making his way from Mansfield, Ohio, to his home in Monroe, North Carolina. Henry thought how good it would be to get some food and a good night's sleep. After exiting Interstate 40 in Winston-Salem, he stopped at a service station at First Street and Hawthorne Road. He used his last fifty cents to buy a drink and a cake. Henry told the attendant that he was broke, had nowhere to stay, and was tired and sleepy. After listening to Henry's sad story, the attendant gladly gave the homeless man directions to the Rescue Mission. Henry followed those directions, and that cool night in September, he found a warm welcome at the Rescue Mission.

Henry Hinson

Later, Henry told the staff more about his life. He was born August 17, 1923, the first of five children to John and Eulalia Hinson, in the little town of Monroe, North Carolina. His mother gave birth to him in a small house behind the Crooked Creek Primitive Baptist Church. The family faithfully attended that church every fourth Sunday. Henry said, "That was the only time we had preaching." After finishing the eighth grade, Henry quit school to help his dad, who was a carpenter by trade and part-time farmer.

(Henry liked to help us chop corn on the Mission farm occasionally because it reminded him of helping his dad.)

In 1943, Henry was called to serve his country in the United States Army. It was there that he began to drink alcohol with the boys. After his discharge—about 1946—he returned home to help his dad on the farm. In 1950, he got a job with Canon Mills in Kannapolis, North Carolina. He worked there sixteen years cutting towels and driving a fork lift. At an early age, having been taught by his dad, Henry had learned to play banjo and guitar. In the years he worked with Canon Mills, he became more involved in playing music and drinking. The first time Henry played professionally was with the Dixie Troubadours in 1961.

Following a disagreement at work, Henry left his job with Canon Mills. He roamed around the country for a while and ended up in Mansfield, Ohio. While in Ohio Henry did not communicate with his family. They later told me that for years they did not know where he was. In 1970, Henry left Ohio and headed back to North Carolina. He was coming through Winston-Salem, headed home, when he found the place he would call home for many years.

After being at the Mission several months, Henry realized he was not sure of his salvation. In February 1971, he trusted Christ as his personal Savior after hearing a message by Rev. Larry Brown. Later, he was baptized at Gospel Light Baptist Church, where Rev. Brown was the associate pastor.

"What is the difference now?" I asked him. Henry replied, "My life is changed. I have a real interest in reading God's Word, and I have a greater interest in the Mission and its ministry." By that time, he had gotten in touch with his family and had been to visit them. His brothers would come to visit him at the Mission. They were grateful that Henry was stable, sober, and serving the Lord at the

Mission. Henry had "anchored his soul in the haven of rest to sail the wild seas no more," as the old song says.

Henry began to grow in the Lord. Later, he became our night watchman. He said, "Night watching gives me time to meditate on God's Word and pray." Henry had very neat, legible handwriting, which made it easy for the staff to read the names on the roster the next morning. He completed a Bible correspondence course and received a certificate of accomplishment. Henry frequented the prayer room the Mission provided to encourage men to have their prayer time. He faithfully requested prayer for his niece, Sharon Hinson, who had developed muscular dystrophy.

Henry and I ate a lot of lunches together, over which we talked about the activities he had to deal with during the night. I took him to visit his family in Monroe several times. His family became personal friends of mine, and when his mother passed away Barbara and I went to her funeral.

Henry loved his job at the Mission and served faithfully for more than twenty-five years. He never drank again, and he never had the urge to ramble again. His family would come to visit him, and he was always welcomed when he went home for Christmas. They were proud of the Christian life their loved one now lived. When his health began to fail, his family gladly took him home with them. Henry realized that his sister-in-law was not able to care for him and Sharon, so he asked his brother to take him to visit several rest homes to see if one would be suitable for him. They decided on Union Park Assisted Living, and he spent his remaining years in his home town. The family told us that he would check all the exit doors at the assisted living home every night to be sure they were locked. Barbara and I went to see him several times.

Henry was a faithful watchman, caring for the men who came to the Mission for help while the staff was sleeping. I thank the Lord for the memories I have of this special man and look forward to seeing him in Heaven.

* * *

Tom Hester grew up in Winston-Salem and went to church every Sunday. As a young man, he accepted Christ as his Savior, but he began to rebel against what he knew was right. At the age of sixteen, he began to drink. Tom said that, from that time on, he began to live one hundred percent for the devil.

After graduating from R. J. Reynolds High School, Tom continued his reckless and carefree lifestyle. His parents divorced, after which Tom lived with his dad. Tom's mother, who was a nurse, died, and his dad remarried bringing a step-mother into the mix. Tom's dad worked for the R. J. Reynolds Tobacco Company for almost forty years. He was a perfectionist and, no doubt, an excellent worker. But young Tom was not diligent to do as his dad wished, which caused conflict in the home. When Tom began his drinking, which caused more problems and disruption in the home, it became unbearable, so Tom left.

Tom had sisters who loved him and tried to help him as much as they could, but they could not stop him from drinking. Tom first came to the Rescue Mission in 1970 when he was twenty-five years old and continued to come for thirty-three years.

Tom said, "All the problems I have had in my life were all related to alcohol. Many times I could have died, but God protected me through it all." He was a willing worker, but when the notion hit him, he would leave to go drink. He knew he could not come back to the Mission for two weeks. His sisters wanted him to stay at the Mission, but he would not stay very long before he would be out there drinking again.

Tom married Donner Sapp in 1980, and soon afterward got a job at a local furniture factory, where he worked for fifteen years in the boiler and finishing rooms. Tom said he was hoping to work there until he retired, but the company unexpectedly went out of business. After this setback in his life, Tom worked at various temporary jobs when he was able to find one. When he was out of work, his drinking got worse. Between jobs, he would end up at the Mission. He would get sober and work awhile, but he could not stay sober on his own. Tom and Donner had one daughter, Christy. Some years later Donner had to be put in a rest home because Tom could not take care of her health problems. Tom always appreciated what the Mission and his sisters did for him and said, "I don't know what I would have done without my sisters; they stood by me through it all."

Tom came to the Mission in November 1993, but this was to be different. Now fifty-eight years old, he had made up his mind that when he checked in this time, he was ready to turn his life over to the Lord and ask the Lord to help him stay sober. As of this writing, Tom has remained sober all these years. He is sixty-eight years old and lives in the Senior Foster Care Division at the Mission. He works taking care of the flowers and shrubs.

Mrs. Anne Parsons, wife of Dan Parsons, the former Director, says, "It [was] refreshing to drive into the Mission's parking lot and see beautiful blooms of purple, orange and yellow peeping through the melting snow. The flowers, donated to the Mission by the City Parks and Recreation Department, were planted by Tom Hester, a Mission resident. Tom loves to work outside and enjoys seeing the results of his hard work." Tom spends his days around the Mission doing yard work or anything he is asked to do to help the Mission.

"I need to stay busy," says Tom. "You have heard that old saying, 'An idle mind is the devils workshop'. I have certainly found that true in my life. I am grateful for the many ways that God has used the Winston-Salem Rescue Mission to help me. I appreciate how the Mission teaches men to live the Christian life and the way the Mission staff members treat the men." Tom attends chapel and Bible classes at the Mission and goes to Gospel Light Baptist Church, where he also attends the Reformers Unanimous.

Tom Hester with his sister

Until her death in September 2012, Tom was faithful to visit Donner in the rest home. I have talked to two of his sisters about their brother and the change in his life in the past ten years. Emily, the oldest lives in Raleigh, North Carolina, and says, "I am so proud of my brother and the change in his life." She loves to visit him at the Mission. The youngest sister, Fay, lives in Winston-Salem. I have talked to her through the years about her concern for her brother and how much she loved him. She has cried and prayed for Tom for forty years and says she had about given up on him. Now she thanks the Lord that she has a sober, loving, and caring brother of whom she is proud.

These sisters say they are so thankful for the miracle the Lord performed in their brother's life at the Rescue Mission. Please don't give up praying for your loved one. He or she may be the next one who will surrender to our Lord. These are real people, with real hurts, whom God has helped.

1974

Harley Reeves came to the Mission in 1974, homeless, unemployed, and separated from his wife and family. He worked for the Mission for a few months and then he took a job as a parking lot attendant, working for a friend of the Mission. Eventually, his family was restored and he and his wife became members of a local church. Harley thanks all those who support the Mission so it could be there when he was in need. Thank the Lord for restoring Harley and his family.

1975

Luther Wilson, a painter by trade, came into the Mission many times; however, he seldom stayed very long. He was a likable man, but like so many of our clients, he was a practicing alcoholic. July 5, 1975, was the beginning of a stay that was to be different. Eight months later he was not only sober but had also rededicated his life to Christ and taken on work responsibility rather than just returning to the streets.

Luther directed the renovation and decorated the four apartments upstairs in the old Mission building on Trade Street. He restored and refinished furniture in the warehouse. This man left many signs of his talents around the Mission. But the real thing that stood out was the change in his attitude. He expressed a real desire to serve the Lord. He attended extra prayer services and Bible studies. He often requested prayer for his family members who had seemingly forgotten him. Eventually, he rebuilt the relationship with his family. His son and his family joined Meadowview Baptist Church where Luther attended and planned to join.

Luther Wilson

I remember Luther giving his testimony in the chapel services at the Mission. He thanked the Lord for saving him and said that, if he ever took another drink, he prayed God would strike him down. Luther stayed straight for several years, but then he took a drink. He fell down in the street and could not get over the curb onto the sidewalk. He was taken to the hospital and diagnosed as having suffered a stroke.

After a stay in the hospital, Luther went to a rest home where he could get therapy. He wanted to come back to the Mission, but he was never able to walk again without assistance. I am glad our God is the God of second chances; He can forgive and restore our joy, but He does not always restore our health. I visited Luther and prayed with him on occasion, but he lived only a few months until he went to meet his Maker. The lesson to be learned is: Be careful how you pray; God may answer your prayers exactly as you prayed.

1976

Archie and Ernestine Tate were the only couple to have an apartment at the Rescue Mission. I became acquainted with them a few years after I arrived in Winston-Salem. Archie and I were the same age, and we were always good friends even though he frequented the services of the Mission. Tina, as Mrs. Tate was called, was a humble lady whom I never saw under the influence of alcohol. Archie, on the other hand, drank for years. Tina followed her husband on the streets of Winston-Salem. She did not have a home, and that did not seem to bother Archie.

Archie and Tina Tate

After the Rescue Mission opened a ladies division, Tina realized she could check into the Mission, but she feared for Archie being on the street alone. Archie, like most of the men with whom we worked, was a decent man when he was sober, but staying sober was a battle he had never won up to that point. I had seen him passed out on the sidewalk. I'd call the police and ask them if there was anything they could do. They, in turn, asked me, "Is he bothering anybody?" Of course, I would have to say, "No." Their reply was, "We are not going to bother him." I was frustrated with their response. I then realized that, if he was not breaking any laws, they had no charges against him.

Archie was not belligerent or disagreeable when he drank, but rather he was humble and apologetic. After years of living on the streets off and on, Tina finally had about all she could take. She checked into the Mission and was thrilled with the warmth of the staff and being in the clean facility—something that she was not accustomed to. She began to read her Bible and talk to the director, Margaret Hemric. Tina got her heart right with the Lord and began to pray for Archie.

When Archie would come into the Mission, all he was interested in was the Lord getting him over that episode with the bottle. As it was said at the Mission, "He would stay long enough to get the wrinkles out of his stomach, and then he was ready to get back out on the street again."

I had learned early on that I couldn't stop a drunk from drinking. He has to get sick and tired of being sick and tired, then he will be more likely to get serious about wanting help. I never heard of an alcoholic who stopped drinking permanently until he wanted to stop bad enough to try anything. If an alcoholic trusts the Lord as His Savior, he does not go back and socialize with the same people at the same places. "Therefore if any man be in Christ, he is a new creature: old things have passed away; behold, all things are become new." (2 Cor. 5:17) He has to get new friends in new places who don't encourage the old life. I have heard many a man say when he first came into the Mission, "I am never going to take another drink." Later he'd say, "If I do take a drink...." and then, "When I take another drink...."

That was when I knew it was just a matter of time until he'd be back out there with the old crowd. I remember one occasion when Archie was drinking and stepped on a round, Roma Rocket™ wine bottle. He fell and broke his ankle. He was on crutches for weeks. That did not stop him from drinking.

Archie told it this way, "I think of the many times I came to the Rescue Mission. Each time I heard the message of the Lord, but I never let Him in my heart. I knew about Him in my head, but I did not want Him in my heart. But, in July 1976, the Lord spoke to my heart, and I promised Him not that I'd stop drinking, but I promised Him I would serve Him if He came into my life and saved me. I had something more important than drinking to do now. Then I was able to get closer to the Lord with the help of Mr. Wilcox, Mr. Franklin, Larry Witt, David Parsons and David Moxley. I now know, without a doubt, that one day I will see my Savior Jesus Christ.

Then the Lord led me to attend night school classes at Piedmont Bible College. My wife and I go to Parkland Baptist Church where Pastor Tilley and our Christian friends have wonderful fellowship together. I have an apartment here at the Rescue Mission where my wife and I can feel secure surrounded by my Christian friends."

Tina tells it this way, "The Lord, through the Rescue Mission, has brought my husband and me back together in a livable situation for the first time in eight years". You could see how II Corinthians 5:17 was lived out in the Tates' lives. Archie was given the opportunity to speak in group sessions and encourage other addicted people.

Archie and Tina eventually moved out of the Mission and had some good years together.

* * *

Alphonso Hines, a twenty-four year old man who had been wounded during his year and a half tour of duty in Vietnam, still had metal fragments in his body. As a result of his wound he was partially disabled and could not work.

Al came to the Mission because he had been robbed and had no place to stay. He had been saved before going into the military, but he had turned his back on the Lord and wandered in sinful living. On February 15, 1976, he rededicated his life to the Lord, and the change in his life was very noticeable. He helped sand furniture in our shop until he found a job at Piedmont Feed and Seed store on Trade Street. Six months later, Al moved into his own apartment. Mr. John Newsome, his employer, said, "He is an exceptionally good employee in spite of his injury."

Alphonso Hines (right) with John Newsome

While I was still the director, I checked the statistics and found that forty-five percent of the men in the Mission were military veterans.

1978

James Rentz was born February 6, 1931, in Fort Meade, Florida. He grew up during the depression years, and when he was only ten years old, James had to cope with the death of his dad. He found himself poor, in despair, and lonely as his mother had to seek employment. The youngest of six children — three boys and three girls — James soon quit school to find work to help support the family.

Circulating among the wrong crowd, James was soon drinking and indulging in the pleasures of the world. He then met Ruth, a young lady who became his wife and the mother of his two children. He was hoping marriage would help curb his drinking problem, but it only became worse and the marriage dissolved.

Roaming from town to town across the United States, James found no peace — only the constant problems brought about because of his lifestyle. He became disillusioned and discouraged and he felt little reason to live. But on July 16, 1978, he met a preacher named W. L. White in Lakeland, Florida. According to James, this faithful preacher revealed to him the plan of salvation and led him to Christ. As James said in his testimony, he was not made perfect that day, but he knew in his heart that he didn't want to do the things he once did. He had hit the bottom in his life and was searching for peace and found it in Christ Jesus

Three days later James left Florida a saved man, but he had little knowledge of the Word of God. With no instructions, he was like a little chick that had wandered from the nest. The man was tired and hungry, and he had no place to lay his head. Besides the clothes on his back and the shoes on his feet, he carried all he owned in a brown paper bag. With these conditions weighing heavy on his mind, in October 1978, James ended up in Winston-Salem, North Carolina, where he was directed to the Winston-Salem

Rescue Mission. James found warmth in the kindness of the staff as they welcomed him with open arms. The staff was eager to meet his immediate needs of food and clothing, and they promised a bed for the night. When James told us of his trusting Christ in July of that year, he was assured that he came to the right place—a place where he would be nurtured and taught the Word of God.

James was introduced to the new convert's class—later called the Mission Christian Fellowship—where he was taught how to live the Christian life that gave him the joy and peace that he had been seeking for so long. With his new relationship with Christ and the Christian fellowship he came to know, James began to enjoy being at the Mission. He soon realized that he did not need the alcohol and all that was involved with that lifestyle. He, along with other Mission converts, later enrolled in a Bible correspondence course and received a certificate for completing the program. James soon started attending church and began to tell others what had happened to him at the Mission.

As soon as he was rested and ready, we assigned James a job. His business skills became self-evident when he started selling goods in the Mission store. As a result, he eventually became the store manager.

James' daughter came up from Fort Meade and visited him, which was very encouraging. We soon realized that James was a special person to whom the Lord had given a real love for the Mission and the men we served. Although he had a withered hand, he could do a lot with one hand. James had management skills, and he loved to work with the men. Even though he still lived at the Mission, we put him on salary, which encouraged him greatly. Some years later we opened another store and made him a general manager over both stores.

James met a lady, Nora, who had stayed at the Mission when we had a Ladies' Division. They were married and moved out on their own. By this time, we had a farm, and I let him raise two calves that we butchered when they were big enough. He would get the meat from one, and the Mission would get the other. He and Nora attended a good church regularly and were growing in the Lord. Nora worked in a part-time job separating clothing at the Mission store, which helped them financially.

James and Nora Rentz

In a few years the Rentzes purchased a house on the north side of town near their church. It was so special for this man, who had come to the Mission with little more than the clothes on his back, to be able to buy his own home. You could see the radiance on their faces and sense the excitement about what the Lord had done for them in their few years together. James and Nora both had grown children from previous marriages whom they enjoyed inviting to come visit them. People in their church and neighbors who knew their testimony were encouraged by their life of service to the Lord. James was invited to give his testimony at different churches and at the Rescue Mission anniversary service. There were some men who came through the Mission and made a commitment to the Lord and never looked back—James Rentz was such a man. James and Nora were faithful in their work at the Mission and in their dedication to their church.

The Mission provided medical insurance for the staff, and the last time James had a medical examination to renew his insurance our agent advised me that James' health was not good. James asked me to handle his estate, if he passed before Nora, and see that she was cared for properly. On October 14, 1996, James suffered a massive heart attack and did not survive. He had been with the Mission more than fourteen years and faithfully served the Lord and the Mission.

Soon after James passed, Nora was diagnosed with cancer and was in the hospital for several weeks. Her children came and helped, along with hospice, until she went home to be with her Lord in 1997. I was asked to be part of both funerals, during which I comforted the family with encouraging words from the testimonies of their loved ones. I look forward to seeing this special couple in heaven.

1979

David Travis was born December 31, 1945, in Pittsburgh, Pennsylvania. A victim of a broken home and a broken marriage, David soon found himself traveling from town to town, job to job, looking for a purpose in life and a reason for living. Somehow his pathway extended itself into Winston-Salem, where he was to experience the loss of yet another job and also the loss of his self-respect. He wandered about the streets day and night trying to blot out the awful misery and sorrow that had gripped his soul. To him, it seemed as if the only thing that would relieve the headache and heartache of life was the bottle. David soon discovered the bottle did nothing for his problems, it only increased their intensity. With no happiness, no joy, and no peace of mind, the thoughts of suicide soon began to grow in this man's mind. He felt at this time in his life no one cared for him; no one was interested in his welfare. Then, an eventful day in the life of David Travis occurred on August 28, 1979. While walking the streets of Winston-Salem, he was told about the Winston-Salem Rescue Mission. He made his way to the Mission where he was made welcome, and his physical needs were met. He informed the staff member on duty that all he wanted was a meal, some clothes, and to spend one night. But, as he stated in his testimony, he later found this place dedicated to God – a place of warmth with a staff who cared and a God Who could save.

David Travis with his mother

David trusted Christ that day as his personal Savior. He had found a place of refuge in the arms of a loving Savior. The grace of God is able to save to the uttermost and, as someone once said, to the gutter most, those who will come unto Christ. Soon after his conversion he began telling the staff what had happened to him. With tears coming down his cheeks, he hugged their necks, and we rejoiced together. David became a great asset in the work of the Rescue Mission. He was a fervent witness to others of God's grace. He became a member of the Mission trio, a singing group, and a student at Piedmont Baptist College evening school. Only God could change the life of this man in such a manner.

David had a mother who never gave up on him, and God had answered her prayers. The staff at the Rescue Mission rejoiced that God had allowed them to have a part in the life of David Travis.

* * *

James H. Blanchard was born October 7, 1923, on a farm in Clinton, South Carolina. His formal education ceased at the eighth grade in order for him to help with chores at home. Raised in a home with Christian parents, James recalled the many times his parents would take him to an old-fashioned church that was warmed by a potbelly stove. There the pastor preached the Word of God.

But he rejected the Gospel, and when he was sixteen, he began to patronize the local pool hall. At the enticement of his peers, he began to indulge himself with the pleasures of the world. By the age of forty-eight he had suffered the heartbreak of having a broken marriage, physical complications brought on by persistent drinking, and a ten-year prison sentence for a felony charge. By the time he was fifty-four, James had developed emphysema, as well as other physical problems brought on by alcohol abuse. James lost his job at the textile mill. At this point, he found himself not only without a regular job, but also he was sometimes homeless, hungry, and feeling helpless and without hope. Over the next two years he wandered from place to place, often bumming change from people so that he could get a mouthful of food or a drink. He eventually came to Winston-Salem and walked the streets a while until someone told him he should go to the Rescue Mission.

James showed up at the Mission on July 12, 1979, hungry, dirty, tired, and discouraged. He was checked in and given food, a shower, clean clothes, clean bed, and the plan of salvation. James showed no interest in salvation, and after a few days, he returned to the streets. Fifteen minutes after he left the Mission two men robbed him of the five dollars he had and inflicted him with five stab wounds — three in the chest and two in the back. He was left to die on the street. Fortunately, the police found him and called an ambulance; he was rushed to the emergency room. James went immediately into surgery. The doctor later told him he was within minutes of death when he was brought in. Sadly, the doctor also informed him he had terminal cancer. James wanted to come back to the Mission where he had felt the concern and warmth of Christian compassion.

After only a few days following his return to the Mission, during the evening service, James came down the aisle, and a personal worker took him to the prayer room where James trusted Christ as his Savior. As he bowed his head in the prayer room, with tears running down his weather-beaten face, he asked Jesus to save him from his sins. Then he thanked God for his father and mother who took him to church when he was a boy.

After all those years, the prayers of his parents had been answered. A man who had escaped physical death had now escaped eternal death by trusting Christ. In the time he had left in his earthly life, James was a changed man. Within a few months, the cancer took its toll and James went on to be with his Lord. This was another miracle in the ministry of rescue in Winston-Salem, North Carolina. To God be the glory.

1980

Holland Hargett was born in Weddington, North Carolina, in May 1924. He was the younger of twins, being born fifteen minutes after his brother. At six-weeks old, he weighed two and a quarter pounds and his "older brother" weighed two and three-quarters pounds. Soon he was diagnosed with curvature of the spine—one of many physical problems he developed.

As a teenager Holland started drinking alcohol to be like his peers, in part, because he was sensitive of his stature.

Holland Hargett

Four feet ten inches was the tallest he became. He quickly went from drinking a few beers to drinking the strong stuff. Despite his physical problems and his drinking, Holland managed to get a job in the Pentagon. His job as a clerical worker put additional stress on him. He eventually went back to Charlotte and worked in the office of a trucking firm until 1973. He was still drinking heavily when he broke his arm. Five years and five operations later his arm healed, but his work skills were reduced by his drinking and physical deterioration.

Holland came to the Mission in November 1978. He checked in and out the same day. Before he left, a staff member witnessed to him and said Holland seemed confused. Then he wandered out of the Mission saying he was going back to Charlotte. Holland returned to the Mission six months later, but he continued to check in and out until January 1980. That January day, when he checked in, was unforgettable. Holland said the best thing that ever happened to him took place at the Mission that day. The staff on duty led him to the Lord. Holland turned his life over to the Lord. Now knowing where he would spend eternity, he had the assurance that the Lord would be with him the rest of the way.

I visited Holland in the Big Elm Retirement Center in Kannapolis, North Carolina, on July 4, 1984, and he told it this way, "I gave my life to the Lord, and it seemed to me that everything in the whole world just changed around me." The Scripture has truly been evidenced in his life. "… old things are passed away; behold, all things are become new." (2 Cor. 5:17b) It was a privilege for my wife and me to visit my friend, who was then sixty years old. His legs could not support his ninety-six pound body, so he was restricted to a wheelchair. He had dealt with cancer but still he smiled. With quivering lips, he told how God changed his life and gave him the hope of Heaven in January 1980 at the Winston-Salem Rescue Mission. What a miracle God can perform in the lives of the homeless and hurting, as well as the home owners and the healthy, if they will invite Him in and surrender their lives to Him.

1981

Gene H. Nelson first came to the Mission in 1968. For many years, Gene was the usual Mission client. In fourteen years, he was in and out of the Mission eighteen times. A combination of alcoholism, emotional problems, and unemployment frequently left him without food and shelter and at the mercy of the streets. When he checked into the Mission, he usually ended up at the warehouse sorting clothes. Sometimes he would stay with us for several months and do very well. Then we would see deterioration in his work habits and loud, blusterous talking. Soon he would have to go to the Reynolds Hospital for care, and then he would come back to the Mission or some other similar care facility to survive.

In October 1981, Gene realized he had a deep problem that all of man's efforts had failed to solve. He trusted Christ as his personal Savior. The change that came about in Gene's life was very obvious to the staff and outsiders who knew him. He came into my office and told me of his desire to serve the Lord, after more than fifty years of serving himself and Satan. We rejoiced together at God's working in his life. He asked me to forgive him for things he said about me and the Mission when he was drinking or emotionally unstable. The humble spirit that radiated from Gene convinced even would-be skeptics that this was a different man from the one who had frequented the Mission over those past fourteen years.

Gene H. Nelson

On March 7, 1982, Gene went to the warehouse where he had faithfully tried to do his part, off and on over the years. We were all shocked when Gene fell dead of a heart attack. He never groaned but had a peaceful look that seemed to say, "I have finished my course and gone home."

This was one of the clearest examples of "rescue the perishing, and care for the dying" I witnessed in my many years of ministry in the Winston-Salem Rescue Mission. To God be the glory, great things He has done.

* * *

Robert Thompson was saved in 1960 at Miller Road Baptist Church in Garland, Texas, where he was also baptized. Robert came to the Mission in March 1981. It had been three years since he had alcohol to drink, and he wanted to keep it that way. He checked into our Senior Foster Care Division for the elderly and disabled.

Robert Thompson

Robert was an inspiration to the staff and residents at the Mission. He never gave up his zeal for living. He had a willing heart and would do anything he could for the Mission. Robert had worked on lawn mowers and small engines and helped us when we needed to get our fork lift motor running. He wouldn't even let the snow stop him from running errands for a few men that were less fortunate than he.

In 1941, Robert was in a severe automobile accident. He was in a coma for a month and a half. It is a miracle that he survived. One of his jugular veins was cut, and his left leg had compound fractures. The doctors tried to save his leg but could not. When his leg was amputated, he had to stay in a body cast for a year and a half. Robert went through twenty operations on the leg, yet we did not see him as a handicapped person. After coming to the Mission, Robert was in the hospital six times — several times for a weak heart and for pneumonia.

Many times we as Christians feel like we have been done wrong by God and others. Robert learned that, while we may not understand, God does not make any mistakes in His plan. If we surrender our lives to Him and serve Him, we know He will never leave us nor forsake us. Robert said, "Without God, I could not have gone through what I have. The Lord has always made a way for me since my accident." What a testimony to the sufficiency of the Lord. It is a blessing to see the Lord leading hurting humanity to a harbor of hope like the Rescue Mission that is supported by a caring community. Thank you for continuing support so that more men like Robert can be rescued.

* * *

Dennis Travis was working in Roanoke, Virginia, where he was a day superintendent for a company with 284 apartments. He decided he needed more money, so he started his own body and fender garage. With both jobs, he was really making it big, but the Lord had other thoughts. All of a sudden, the bottom fell out from under Dennis. He couldn't make ends meet.

Dennis was raised in an area of Virginia where there seemed to be a lot of access to alcohol. As a result, Dennis said, "I was an alcoholic by the time I was twelve." His brother, David, had also become an alcoholic at a very early age. David had come to the Rescue Mission two years earlier and trusted Christ as his Savior. As he began to grow in the Lord, David became burdened for Dennis. David had the opportunity to witness to Dennis when they were visiting their mother in Virginia. David tried to plant the seed of God's Word in his brother's heart and prayed for him.

Now that Dennis had lost everything, he began to think about something his brother had said to him. David said, "I don't need pills or alcohol anymore; I have the Lord Jesus Christ." With no money and no place to call home, Dennis went back to visit his mother. There he happened to see his brother again. David reminded him of the Rescue Mission where he could get some real help. Dennis came to the Mission on September 13, 1981, and turned his life over to Christ. It was no easy decision. Dennis said, "I fought it till I had no fight left." David and his mom had been praying for Dennis for two years and they rejoiced greatly in their prayers being answered. Then Dennis joined David and their mother in praying for another brother, Riley, who needed Christ.

* * *

Seven years after John Cuffle left the Mission, he sent the following letter to David Parsons, a former staff member:

Dear David,

For some reason the Lord reminded me of you, from the time I lived at the rescue mission in 1974-1975. At that time you knew me as John Abril, which wasn't my real name. I had been on the run from the law for some time. In June 1975, I was arrested, after a year on the run. I was sentenced to 125 years in prison.

I was really affected by the services the mission had, and many times I wanted to come forward and accept Christ. But I didn't because I was living the life of a lie under a false name and wanted for armed kidnapping and murder.

In a Utah prison in 1976 I took a Bible study for a year but still didn't accept Christ. In December of 1980, I finally accepted Christ and was baptized here at Walla Walla. I go to services every week, and Bible study every Wednesday.

I hope your life is filled with goodness and you are living ever stronger for the Lord each day. My brother in Phoenix, Arizona, hasn't written in months, and my sister in Las Vegas writes once in a while. I really got to like the people at the mission, but things were so messed up for me I really wasn't as nice as I should have been towards people. I have been trying to find people to write to and send pamphlets to so I can witness for our Lord and Savior.

I keep praying for people and hoping their lives will be touched by my prayers and will accept Jesus. Whatever happened to Chris and Tex Ashley who stayed at the mission? I will close and hope to hear from you one of these days.

Your friend and brother in Christ,
John Cuffle

David Parsons

1983

Mr. Harold Siterlit told me his story in 1983. He had made a decision for Christ in 1946. During the years following World War II, he said he had felt lost and disillusioned until he found an anchor in Christ that would hold him securely for the rest of his life.

Mr. Siterlit said, "I have had my ups and downs — physically, financially, and spiritually — but I have always stood on His promises and known that only by His grace I have been able to come this far. As I grow older, I find that I bend more easily to God's wishes and believe that His will is what led me again to the Winston-Salem Rescue Mission. I have been to other missions throughout the country, but few have Christ-oriented programs as strong as the one here. Certainly my work here is rewarding, knowing the talents He bestowed on me are being used for the honor and glory of God.

I am presently working in the kitchen and find the work most enjoyable. Providing more than 4,000 meals a month in these economical times is a great testimony to God's abundance and the tremendous power of prayer. Daily I can see God work in meeting our needs through our prayer and the prayers of those who are faithful and dedicated to the mission. I can see the Spirit of God working in the hearts from the donations of extra frozen foods, meat, and canned goods received from concerned people. I can see the Lord's hand as He blesses our farm, which brings forth beef, pork, and fresh vegetables for our table. God is truly great."

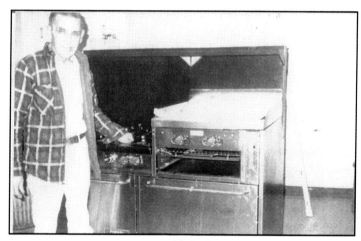

Harold Siterlit

Harold Siterlit was an amazing man. He could take different foods, put them together, season the mixture, and everybody liked it. His heart's desire was to be in a place where he could see the hand of God working and know that he was being used to serve others. Harold lacked only a few hours to get a degree in engineering. He could not only cook, but he could also design and build almost anything he wanted. He could have gotten other jobs outside the Mission, but he felt called to help us. As he said in his testimony, he wanted to be associated with a ministry that did things the way he felt a Christian work should be carried out.

Harold would "pray in food" and then tell us about what the Lord had provided in answer to prayer. He was such a faithful, frugal, dependable, dedicated and caring Christian man. He stayed with us about ten years until his health became a concern. After he retired, he remained in Winston-Salem and kept close ties with the Mission. We sometimes had Ensure™, a dietary supplement, given to us. Rev. Moore, the Public Relations Director, would share it with Harold. Harold often volunteered to come in and cook a holiday meal just to help the Mission. He had no other family besides his Mission family.

I have thanked the Lord for this man's ministry with us through the years. Harold gave himself the title Minister of Food. All who enjoyed his cooking would say, "Amen." To know him was to love him. When he passed away I was called on to officiate at his funeral.

1984

Ed Johnson was born in June 1955 in Richmond, Virginia. When Ed was two-years old, his dad, a diesel mechanic, died of cancer. Ed, along with his mom and sister, moved to Patrick County, Virginia, to start life without his dad. His mother remarried, and they had to adjust to a new dad with whom Ed could not get along. He wanted to be loved and accepted by his parents and friends. Since he could not please his stepfather, he started running away from home, and he sometimes stayed for days with friends who introduced him to alcohol. At the age of thirteen, he was arrested for disorderly conduct; at fifteen he smoked his first marijuana. By this time, he realized that he was searching for something, but he did not understand what it was.

In 1972, Ed met a preacher whom he respected very much, but the preacher got into trouble and disappointed Ed causing him to look elsewhere for spiritual help. (In the mid-1970s, Ed became one of the first people in Patrick County to get involved in the "Jesus Movement.") In 1977, he joined the Army, but after two years he became disenchanted with the service and came home. The feelings of despair and failure in every area of his life drove Ed back to the streets without work or food. Sleeping out like an animal and rejected by his family because of his waywardness brought the thought of suicide into Ed's mind.

In the summer of 1981, he applied for a job washing dishes at Springs of Life Christian Camp. However, because he had no home, he was not given the job, but instead he was recommended to go to the Winston-Salem Rescue Mission. He arrived at the Mission in August, thinking he was coming to a monastery for a few days until he could get back into the Army.

For the next two-and-one-half years, Ed stayed at the Mission off and on—still searching for something he had never found. On April 11, 1983, after living on the streets for two months, dirty, hungry, and hurting, he came to see his friend, Rev. Bill Fryar at the Mission. Once more, Rev. Fryar checked Ed into the Mission and witnessed to him about his need to accept the Lord Jesus Christ as his Savior. Ed made a profession of faith that day, but he did not have complete assurance. As his mind cleared over the next few months, Ed began to understand what he had been searching for was Jesus Christ and that he could trust his life in His hands.

In December 1983, Ed got a part-time job with the prospect of going full time later. His boss was a Christian man who became a great encouragement to him. Ed joined a local church and was baptized. He began to enjoy the fellowship of God's people and studying His Word. Ed gave his testimony to youth groups as an encouragement to young people not to make the same mistakes he had made in his early life. When his stepfather passed away, Ed returned to Virginia to live with his mother.

Ed Johnson

* * *

Paul Adkins was born February 16, 1953, in Germantown, Pennsylvania. His dad was a gambler, and his mom kept alcohol in the home. Both parents were alcoholics. Paul's dad died when Paul was nine years old. His mother remarried, and his stepfather had the same problems as his dad. Paul took his first drink when he was ten years old. He remembered drinking until he passed out and waking up sick. The family argued constantly, which made life uncomfortable for Paul. So, he would take beer from his house and share it with the neighbor boy because they "liked the way it made them feel." By the time he was seventeen years old Paul had been charged with trespassing and public drunkenness on numerous occasions. With things at home getting worse, Paul said that, after thinking it over for a few days, he decided to leave. His parents did not care to have him around so he left home. He picked up odd jobs and bummed around Pennsylvania, sometimes spending time on Vine Street, the skid row of Philadelphia, Pennsylvania.

Eventually, Paul was picked up and sent to the State Hospital for three years because of his arrest record in the state of Pennsylvania. His good behavior earned him an early release; however, he went back to his old habits and was soon in trouble with the police again. This went on for awhile, and finally, the police told him if he would leave the state and not come back, they would let him go; if he did not, he was going back to the State Hospital. Paul chose to leave.

Paul traveled south, eventually arriving in Hickory, North Carolina. One day, while carrying several bottles of vodka in a bag, he saw a ladder against the side of a three-story building. He climbed the ladder to the top of the building, where he was by himself. He drank the vodka until he was completely intoxicated. At some point, he decided to go to the edge of the building and look down at the road below. The next thing he remembered he was waking up in the hospital in Hickory with a broken back, abrasions, and bruises. After a month in the local hospital, he was flown to the North Carolina Baptist Hospital in Winston-Salem where he stayed for months. When the hospital determined he was ready to be released, they called the Mission.

It was not unusual for the hospital to call us and arrange for a homeless person being released to come to the Mission. We were cautious not to accept someone who needed medical care that we were neither equipped nor staffed to provide. However, we wanted to help the other agencies if possible. We had to look at each individual case and decide on the basis of their needs. The hospitals,

Veterans Administration, and the alcohol treatment facility frequently referred their clients to the Mission. They knew that those clients would receive, at no cost, housing, food, and counseling until they could survive on their own. This happened regularly when a person was from out of town and had no resources or relatives to call on for help. We felt the Lord had prepared a place where the weak, weary, and wounded who were tired of wandering, could find help and hope. But we had limitations when it came to helping those with medical needs.

The Mission checked Paul in and gave him clothes, a clean bed, food, and a Christian witness to pray with him and try to help him get his life on track. Paul did not know what Christian love was. He went to the services and was counseled many times. He appeared to be a loner and had little to say, choosing to stay to himself. After some time, he wanted something to do. We found that he was able to sit in a chair and sort clothes at the warehouse. As Paul gained strength, he wanted to help on the cardboard truck. This was a crew that used a ton and a half truck to pick up flattened cardboard boxes from the grocery stores and take them to the Paper Stock Dealer. A long chain was wrapped around the cardboard so it could be pulled off the truck by a tow motor. No manpower was needed to unload it.

Paul seemed to be reasonably content, and he received some money for his personal needs. If he had wanted to, he could have gone out and looked for a job. His body had healed somewhat. Paul never complained, and he did what he could do for the Mission. Later, when the Mission acquired a farm in Davie County, Paul went out to the farm and lived in a mobile home so he could help me care for the animals, which he enjoyed very much. We had a phone in the mobile home so that I could call him every morning at 7 a.m., and we would discuss the concerns I had for the day. I went to the farm on Wednesday and Saturday mornings to take Paul his supply of food and check on things. On Saturday, I would take Paul to the grocery store to get his personal items; afterward, we went to lunch and discussed the work that needed to be done on the farm. It was a time I had to witness to him and help him develop a relationship with the Lord. This went on for a number of years.

Paul Adkins with Ryan Beadles (Wilcox's grandson)

After I retired, Paul's health began to deteriorate, so he moved back to the Mission. He had arthritis and emphysema, which eventually resulted in him having to be on oxygen day and night. He moved into Senior Foster Care Division, the hall for retirees and disabled persons. There the staff monitored his condition. When he was asked about his relationship with the Lord, he assured the staff and visitors that he had gotten his heart right with the Lord in 2001 and that he read his Bible regularly. When the staff visited his room, his Bible was always close to his chair. Then Paul became too weak to function in the Mission, so arrangements were made for him to stay in the local hospice facility. After two months he was transferred to a nursing facility. Chaplain Mullins visited him every week, and Mrs. Mullins prepared a birthday cake for Paul's last birthday. Some of his friends from the Mission visited Paul on the occasion. The last time I visited Paul, in February 2012, I took him a bag of his favorite candy, M&Ms™. He assured me he was ready to meet his maker. I had prayer with him for the last time during that visit.

April 26, 2012, Paul went home to be with his Lord. Chaplin Mullins made arrangements for the burial by getting a funeral home to prepare the body and a church to donate a grave plot. Chaplin Mullins officiated at the grave-side service. What would Paul's life have been like without the Rescue Mission? Paul Adkins found purpose, peace, and a place that cared for him when he could not care for himself. There are thousands more Paul Adkins in this world—lonely, weak, weary, wounded, and wondering if God has a place for them. Rescue Missions across this country have open doors for the hungry, homeless, and hurting.

* * *

1986

Nathaniel Alexander was born in Winston-Salem on November 15, 1944. Because of his mother's poor health, Nathaniel—or "Sleepy" as he was nicknamed—went to live with his Christian grandmother, who greatly influenced his life.

During grade school, it was learned that Sleepy had a problem with his hands. He would often drop heavy objects because of the pain that would shoot up his arms, he also had seizures.

After a few years in school, he was transferred to special education. When Sleepy was eighteen years old, he quit public school and went into training for the handicapped where he was given the opportunity to learn trades, from shoe repair to kitchen work. At last Sleepy finished the course in kitchen work and was hired at a restaurant in the city.

Eventually, the problem with his hands resulted in several stacks of dishes being dropped. After several restaurants had tried to work with him, it became evident that he could not make it in the workplace. Due to his disabilities, Sleepy applied for disability and began receiving a disability check when he was in his early twenties. It was about this time in his life when he made a profession of faith at his grandmother's church. Soon, the men in his neighborhood began coming to his house on Sunday mornings and talking Sleepy out of going to church. Then they started bringing him booze and encouraging him to go with them. Whenever his check came, they expected him to share with them. Before long, his life revolved around drinking and partying with his friends. At one point, in desperation, Sleepy thought of drinking a can of Drano™ he had seen in the cabinet. All during this time, his grandmother continued to pray that Sleepy would see the error of his ways.

In 1981, because of drinking, Sleepy got into serious trouble with the law and was sentenced to eight years in prison. He was sent to the Danbury prison unit to serve his time. His dear grandmother prayed faithfully and wrote her loved one regularly. His mother and aunt also sent letters with money to help him. Prayers were being answered. Sleepy began to feel conviction for his sins; and one day, alone in his cell, he poured his heart out to the Lord asking for forgiveness. Right then, peace came to the troubled heart of this sin-sick, broken-hearted, and convicted soul. Bible reading and attending prayer services became very important in the life of this new babe in Christ. Then one day a letter came telling him his grandmother had died and been buried several weeks previously. The one who had always cared for him was gone, and he felt all alone. What would he do when he got out of prison?

On October 14, 1985, while resting in his cell, the voice of the Sergeant called out, "Nathaniel Alexander, pack your belongings, you can go home." Sleepy slipped to his knees and thanked the Lord for early release. Then, the big question, "Where is home?" came to mind. After being released in Winston-Salem, Sleepy went to the home of an aunt who had been kind to him in the past. However, she had a small house and no room for another permanent resident. His mother was in Philadelphia, and that was too far to go. Then he remembered some of the inmates talking about the Mission in Winston-Salem where the homeless were welcomed. Rev. McDaniel checked Sleepy in on October 15, 1985. With the support and encouragement of the Mission, his local church, an encouraging aunt, the local mental health agency, and his

Nathaniel Alexander

faith in the Lord, Sleepy became sober and satisfied with the peace he found that day in prison.

Rev. McDaniel helped Sleepy get his disability check reinstated. With careful management of his funds and taking advantage of the money-saver fares in Winston-Salem, he was able to get a ticket to Philadelphia to see his mother for the first time in several years. What a difference the Mission made in this man's life. Every such man has a story to tell of why his life was in disarray, but our God can do a miracle and put the pieces together again.

1989

Herb Carter grew up on a farm in Henry County, Virginia, in a family of five children, one of whom was his twin brother. In 1954, Herb finished high school and started working in a supermarket. The loss of his dad brought sorrow and grief to the young man. A neighbor gave Herb some amphetamines to help him through the grief of his dad's death. The effect of the pills gave him something

Herb Carter

he liked, and soon he used them as a crutch to help him through the day. In 1960, Herb's addiction led him to despair, and finally, after failing an attempted suicide, he sought help. By 1964, Herb broke the drug habit, but alcohol took its place. For the next fifteen years, he went from job to job and drunk to drunk. Finally, after a run-in with the law and losing his apartment, he decided to come to the Winston-Salem Rescue Mission, which he had visited years before. In November 1989, sad and discouraged, Herb came to us wanting spiritual and physical help.

The Sunday before Christmas, Herb trusted Christ as his personal Savior. His life began to change. Those habits that had hurt him were replaced with hope that healed and helped him through the day. Herb worked as a salesman in the Mission store and operated the cash register. He was a faithful member of Woodland Baptist Church. Herb appreciated those who supported the Mission where he found food, shelter, and a place that cared about his physical and spiritual needs. I attended Herb's funeral some years later, after he had finished his life well, serving the Lord.

1996

For seven years Lynn Holloway lived a homeless, crack-addicted life, in Los Angeles, California; Denver, Colorado; and, finally, Ashville and then Durham, North Carolina, where it all came to an end. In July of 1994, Lynn received his pay check and, as usual, spent it all on crack cocaine. Later that same evening, after he had spent all of his money, Lynn went walking—his destination nowhere and his purpose none. While crossing Hillsborough Street in Durham, North Carolina, he was struck by an automobile. When the Emergency Medical Services and police arrived, Lynn was placed in the ambulance and taken to Duke Hospital Emergency Room. While lying in the back of that ambulance, Lynn called upon the Lord for help, and the Lord Jesus Christ heard his cry.

Upon his release from the emergency room, Lynn was given instructions to report to the Veterans Administration (VA) Hospital for further treatment. It was at the VA Hospital where Lynn was told about the Durham Rescue Mission (DRM). He was given a one-way city bus ticket to the DRM. Upon Lynn's arrival, he was greeted with a warm welcome. Lynn's arm was still in a sling and his shoulder in a body wrap to keep his arm and shoulder stabilized. The supervisor, Gary Steed, told Lynn that the DRM was a working mission. Lynn then replied, "I have one good arm.

I can push a broom." So, in August 1994, Lynn was checked into the Durham Rescue Mission.

August, 3, 1994, Lynn was asked to report to Rev. Crowley's office. Once Lynn was seated, Rev. Crowley opened the Bible and led Lynn in the plan of salvation using the "Romans Road." On that day, by faith Lynn accepted the Lord Jesus Christ as his Savior and Lord over his life. Shortly after Lynn's salvation, he began working as Rev. Crowley's assistant, witnessing and sharing the plan of salvation to other residents. When the residents began asking him Biblical questions he did not know how to answer, Lynn began to pray about getting some Biblical training. He prayed with Rev. Mills and with Rev. Tart about going to Bible College. God laid it on Lynn's heart to attend Piedmont Bible College in Winston-Salem, North Carolina. Rev. Mills knew that Lynn would need employment to pay for tuition. So, he set up a scholarship plan and called me. After speaking with me, Lynn not only had a scholarship for school, but he was also employed with the Winston-Salem Rescue Mission.

Lynn did not know me, and I had only heard of Lynn Holloway, but I did know Rev. Mills. Both of us were instrumental in the Christian walk of Lynn Holloway. In the first of many meetings — business and fellowship — Lynn and I got to know each other. In the fall of 1996, Lynn began his college career and his employment at the Winston-Salem Rescue Mission. The next six years proved to be very fruitful.

While working on his degree during the day, Lynn worked evenings at the Mission, getting the hands-on training and experience needed for the work of the ministry. I always made sure Lynn had enough time to study. We set up a schedule that allowed for classroom time, study time, and work. Lynn's duties and responsibilities included being an assistant to the Chaplain by conducting evening worship services and Bible Study. He directed the weekly Overcomers programs, a program based on Biblical principles, discussed by the clients, but directed by staff. He also helped in checking in new clients and attended staff meetings. When the Rescue Mission purchased a farm in Yadkin County to raise meat and vegetables for the Mission, we also envisioned the farm as a place to help the younger men get their GED and offer counseling, Bible teaching, and training in how to get and hold a job. To that purpose, we developed an educational program and sent Lynn, along with two other staff members, to school in Los Angeles, California, to get special training in how to help the younger men get their education and job training.

Lynn related, "Once a month I returned to Durham to preach at the DRM on Sunday evening. At the end of each service, I was given the evening offering. One day Rev. Wilcox and I were talking about my trip to Durham and he made this statement, 'Lynn, don't always go expecting a blessing, but go and give a blessing; take something with you to give.' We usually had some extra food or garden vegetables to share with our friends in Durham, so from that day on, Rev. Wilcox always made sure I had something to give whenever I went to preach at the DRM."

I truly enjoyed the holidays, Thanksgiving and Christmas. It was a time of the year when the Rescue Mission would receive food donations for the elderly, the sick, and shut-ins. We would take the food out to the homes and it was a blessing to see the joy and gladness on the faces of the people. It allowed them to have a blessed Thanksgiving and Merry Christmas.

I also learned that each rescue mission operated differently, even though they are faith-based ministries. The training and experience I received at the Winston-Salem Rescue Mission has been unforgettable, and I owe it all to a man—Rev. Neal Wilcox—who gave me the opportunity to get the training needed to help change people's lives for our Savior."

Lynn Holloway

It was a blessing to have a part in helping my friend, Lynn Holloway, get his education so that he could be a more effective servant of God.

* * *

Charles King, Jr. came to the Mission in 1996, unemployed, broke, and homeless. He had grown up in Winston-Salem and graduated from R.J. Reynolds high school. His mother, with whom he was very close, passed away when he was seventeen. This seemed to bother him greatly, since he was not as close to his dad. Charles attended North

Carolina Central College in Durham, North Carolina, for a year. Then he came home and stayed with his dad, attending Winston-Salem State University where he received a degree in Sociology. After college Charles went to work at R.J. Reynolds Tobacco Company where his dad had been employed for more than thirty-two years. Charles worked there for twenty years. But, eventually, he was dismissed for drinking. He went to several alcoholic rehabilitation centers, but they did not seem to help his problem. With few options left, he made his way to the Winston-Salem Rescue Mission where he was welcomed and an effort was made to meet his immediate physical needs as well as his spiritual needs.

Charles King, Jr.

Charles was a product of a good family, and other than his problem with alcohol, he dealt with life's issues very well. He had a good personality and was willing to work. He was assigned to the Mission store where he seemed to be a natural at getting along with the customers. Charles soon realized the root of his problem was a spiritual need to trust the Lord for salvation and that the Lord would help him overcome his addiction to alcohol. Once he got things right with the Lord and became a part of a local church, his lifestyle reflected his desire to serve the Lord. The void left in his life when his mom died was now filled with his Lord and Savior, Jesus Christ. Charles was a good witness to his peers at the Mission as well as the customers he served in the store. He eventually moved back with his dad, who lived alone, and they were compatible, now that Charles left the alcohol alone and wanted to serve the Lord.

Charles' family was so proud of him. Now that his life had changed, they felt they had their loved one back. In November 2008, Charles got up and went to his job in the Mission store, but he could not hold his pen steady to write. His arm felt numb. He went back home and told his dad about the numbness in his hand and left side. His dad took him to the Winston-Salem Clinic, and they sent him to the hospital where it was determined he had suffered a stroke. After a three-week stay in the hospital he was transferred to Whitaker Care where he received more therapy. Charles was later released to come home with a tripod cane to help him walk. His elderly dad helped to take care of him.

I called Charles and talked with him at his home. He was never able to come back to work at the Mission. In early August 2011, he went back to the hospital, and on August 27, he went to be with his Lord.

With the help of the Lord through the ministry of the Rescue Mission and his church, this was another soul who found a way out of the liquid jungle of alcohol. Charles became the son, brother, and uncle who his family could respect and appreciate — the result of another miracle in the ministry of rescue. Charles donated his eyes to the eye bank with hopes they would help someone else.

* * *

In 1996, Charles Burrow gave, in his own words, the following as his testimony that God was not finished with him:

Charles Burrow

On February 24, 1996, a Forsyth County Deputy Sheriff brought me from John Umstead hospital to the Winston-Salem Rescue Mission. From September 15, 1994, until I was released from the Umstead hospital I was in three detox centers, three drug and alcohol rehabilitation centers, and twice in Umstead and Duke University Hospitals. It was while I was in Duke Hospital for twenty-four days that the Lord started me on a journey that has led me to where I am now. I was near death at Duke Hospital as a result of my continual drinking. I was having seizures because three blood clots had developed in my brain and one in my neck. The surgeons told my two daughters that I would never live through an operation. However, if by some miracle I should live, I would be a vegetable the rest of my life and would have to have continual care. While in the operating room, I seemed to hear a voice saying, 'go back, your journey is not yet over.'

Up to this point in time, I had lost a good job with the Sara Lee Corporation, my house, my wife, and two new cars, everything I had worked for years all because of alcohol and drugs. Even my two beautiful daughters no longer respected me or wanted anything to do with me.

After I was released from Umstead for the final time, I checked into the Winston-Salem Rescue Mission on February 24, 1996. Five weeks later I walked into an empty church on Fifth Street, placed my hands on the Bible, and asked Jesus Christ to come into my heart. He saved me that day and my life quickly changed. God worked through the staff of the Rescue Mission and I went from a cot on the third floor to being hired as a staff member for the Mission eleven months later.

I now have a beautiful wife, whom I met in my church, a new house in the suburbs, and the blessing of God upon my life. I have my two daughters back and three grandchildren and a life of miracles, including three step-children, a step granddaughter-in-law, and a sweet step-granddaughter. God has given me a complete new family that loves me. God's goodness and blessings never ran out. I can now say with the apostle Paul, "I can do all things through Christ which strengthens me.

Now, seventeen years later, God is still working his magic in my life. After working for fourteen and one-half years at the Rescue Mission, it was time for me to say goodbye and do something else with my life. After four months "rest" I decided to go back to work. A man like me just cannot sit around and do nothing. I worked part-time as a shuttle driver at one of the local car dealerships. After being the route supervisor at the Mission, I had a very good working knowledge of the streets in the area, which was a real asset when I was approached about being a driver for the dealership. Then I had my opportunities to talk to the customers in my van about the Lord. Also, I have had many opportunities to speak with some of the employees about the goodness of God in my life and how God could change their lives too. Many of them have found it almost hard to believe that I was once an alcoholic who had lost everything in life. I have since retired from the dealership, and am seeking God's will for the next step in my life. I know that it will be good as He has always had a great plan for my life.

God has done such a marvelous work in my life. Once I was full of bitterness, sadness, and anger about what life had brought me and now I have sweet peace, joy, and contentment. There continues to be challenges as I am endeavoring to continue growing in Christ. Of course, my life has its problems like everyone else, but I am continuing to learn that God is in control. I can go to Him with my problems and He gives me peace while He is solving the problem or showing me how to solve it. I still love the verse, "And we know that all things work together for good to them that love God, to them who are called according to his purpose." Romans 8:28

With all my heart, I appreciate what God has done in my life, and how He used the Winston-Salem Rescue Mission to bring me to Christ and start the process of change in my life. I love going to church and try to win other people to Christ. For all the wonder that God has done in my life, I give him all the glory and praise.

1998

As written in his own words, the following is the testimony of Harry E. Shultz:

Harry E. Shultz

After spending almost 4 years at the WSRM [Winston-Salem Rescue Mission] from Oct. 1998 to Feb. 23, 2002, this was now the new life where I found my foundation where I found my footing. My councilors during this time were several ministers Rev. Neal Wilcox, Rev. McDaniel, Rev. Moxley, Chaplin Holbert Stephens and Assistant Chaplin Lynn Holloway. Rev. Haynes Moore was my closest friend. The Good Lord chose these clergymen in my life because each one played an important role in my recovery. Rev. Moore was my very close friend and supervisor and mentor, as well as father image in my life at the Rescue Mission while I was there in my recovery from drugs and alcohol. Over the few years I lived at the mission, I felt the call of the Lord to change my life and serve Him. I had many hats as I worked at the Rescue Mission. It all started when Rev. Wilcox ask me to join him and Rev. Moore to have me share my testimony at several churches, as well as colleges and Christian Schools.

After serving in my walk with the Lord Jesus Christ I felt the Lord was leading me back home to Rochester, N. Y. to be with my family and, my wife to be, Kristine Schultz, as well as my children, Victoria, Scott and Kandace. Before I was going to return to my home town there was some things I needed to accomplish first. I needed to speak to my pastor, Doctor Ron Baity first about the Lord calling me to preach. In January of 2002 I accepted the call to the ministry. Now I felt more equipped to go home to my family. I had been searching for some kind of ministry to start back home. When I was in Rochester in the summer of 2001 I applied for a job at the Open Door Rescue Mission. I waited several months before I received a phone call from the Executive Director of the mission, Mr. Ronald Fox, just two weeks before I was to leave the Winston-Salem Mission. The Lord was on time for me to get there and get settled before going to work at the Open Door Mission. How good our God is! So I moved on Feb. 23, 2002 and lived with my sister, Kim, for seven months. She had kept my daughter, Victoria, for 4 years while I was in North Carolina getting my life together. On May 4th, 2003 Kristen and I were married. A year later, May 2, 2004, the Lord blessed us with a healthy baby boy Brent Michel. A week later we bought our first house and shortly after words [sic] we found a strong Independent Baptist Church,

Open Door Baptist church, after searching for 2 years. The Pastors name is Tom Hauser. Today is my 11th anniversary serving the Lord at the counseling center where I council [sic] men on our 12 to 14 month program. It is the best job in the world. My favorite Scripture is James 4:8 "Draw neigh [sic] unto God and God will draw neigh [sic] unto thee. My daughter Victoria blessed us with our first grandson, Seth, May 15, 2011. All that I am and all that I hope and all I possess is the Lords. How good the Lord is. Thank you!

In His service Harry E. Schultz

2001

While the following is the testimony of a man who came to the Rescue Mission after my retirement, I wanted to share with you how our great God reaches out in love to everyone, no matter their circumstance, or how they have lived their life. He is always there for all who seek Him.

Dan Parsons and Chorn Thong

Chorn Thong's testimony

Submitted by Rick Browning

Bethesda Baptist Church

Conover, North Carolina

As a native Cambodian, former Buddhist monk, soldier during the Khmer Rouge, and political refugee, Chorn Thong knew many harrowing experiences and time of deep sorrow, but ultimately great deliverance and victory. Chorn shared with me that on one occasion, he was tied up and placed along with others in the back of a truck. However, before he could be executed, an old man untied him, allowing his escape, but not before Chorn set free several others. He fled to Thailand and eventually was brought to Rhode Island before coming to Conover, North Carolina.

My contact with the family came through his son's attendance at youth events at our church. The first time I met Chorn, he was standing in the hall of the church, obviously intoxicated. When I attempted to share the Gospel with him, he said, "Sir, you help my son. You no help me. It is too late for me." Chorn believed that he was too far gone for even God's help.

Over the course of several years, I had many opportunities to be in his home and share with him the gospel of Jesus Christ. Sitting on the floor in his sarong with his Cambodian Bible laid out before him he followed along as I read passages in English from my Bible. He was always respectful of both the Bible and any servant of the Lord who sought to rescue him. One time upon visiting Chorn I found him preparing to kill a coworker who had made fun of him. After I pleaded with him to abandon his plan, he called the person who was going to take him to kill the man and told him not to come. He then looked at me and said, "Okay sir, I not kill."

When I would attempt to win him to Christ, he would point to the ever-present bottle of alcohol on his kitchen table and say, "Sir, I take that." The trauma of war plagued him, and alcohol was the only way he knew to numb his troubled soul.

But then an overwhelming tragedy came; Chorn's son, Phon (pronounced Pahn) who had professed Christ, fell away from church. Several unsuccessful attempts were made to see him restored to our fellowship. One morning at 2 a.m. I received a call from our local sheriff's department asking if I could come to the Thongs' home. Phon had been next door at a friend's and had been shot and killed.

The most difficult task I have ever had was to awaken Chorn Thong and his wife to tell them that their son was dead. Chorn first stood with questioning unbelief, but when the reality of his cherished son's death grasped him, he rolled on the floor in agony.

Phon's death brought Chorn into a perilous condition. In his despair he decided to end his life by lying down in the road, hoping that he might be run over by an unsuspecting driver. Instead, a kind soul came upon him and called for help. Once again, the Lord mercifully intervened to spare Chorn. He was then admitted to the hospital for observation.

After his release from the hospital, due to threats made during a drunken rage, he wound up in the county jail. At that time, our church conducted a ministry to the inmates in the jail, and there we found a forlorn and haggard Chorn. Obtaining his release, I took him to the Winston-Salem Rescue Mission, where the caring staff welcomed him and began to minister to his body and soul, wrapping his troubled soul in the tender mercies of the Lord. They took him to church where he eventually accepted Christ as Savior.

Chorn returned to his home a new man. His simple testimony was "one God," given with a finger pointed toward heaven. Now free from false religion, the demons of his past, and the bondage of alcohol, he drank the living water, and his soul was abundantly satisfied in Christ.

Chorn's home going came not long after his difficult journey to faith ended. The Lord took him home after only a few brief months back with us. Now I look forward to seeing him in heaven. I sometimes wonder if, when I next see him, Chorn Thong will greet me with a confident expression and one finger pointed upward, triumphantly proclaiming in his rich baritone voice, "One God!"

The following recollections of Chorn's time at the Mission were provided by Hobart B. Stephens, Chaplain, Winston-Salem Rescue Mission, 1995-2005.

Chorn Thong came to the Winston-Salem Rescue Mission from Conover, North Carolina. He had an amazing testimony of God's grace in his life. Shortly after he came to the Mission, I began taking him to my home church, Gospel Light Baptist Church, in Walkertown, North Carolina.

As I remember, after Chorn had attended church for about three months, one Sunday evening following the conclusion of Brother Bobby Roberson's message on salvation, when the invitation was given, Chorn went to the altar on his own without provocation from anyone. I followed him to the altar, and asked him, "Why did you come to the altar?" He replied through his tears, "Me want what he say...me want what he say." Chorn finally realized his need for Christ.

I led Chorn down the "Romans Road" [Romans 3:23, Romans 6:23, Romans 5:8, and Romans 10:9-10] to a saving knowledge of Jesus Christ. When we were finished, Brother Bobby asked me to bring Chorn over so that he could speak with him. Brother Bobby asked Chorn what happened to him. All Chorn could say as he held his Cambodian Bible high above his head and pointed up toward Heaven, "ONE GOD...ONE GOD... ONE GOD!!"

Brother Bobby was crying as he said, "I believe he got that part right...ONE GOD!!" What a blessing to have had a small part in his conversion. One planted, one watered, but God gave the increase.

With blessed assurance, we will see Chorn Thong again...and maybe soon.

LETTERS OF APPRECIATION

---◆---

August 1984

Respect unto the Lowly

By Pastor Bud Owen

*Though the Lord be high, yet hath he respect unto the lowly:
but the proud he knoweth afar off. Ps. 138:6*

From its inception, I have been appreciative of the
Winston-Salem Rescue Mission and the marvelous work
it is doing. Only eternity will reveal the invaluable spiritual
assistance afforded to the men. Not only is spiritual help
given, but also physical and psychological. "Learn to do
well; seek judgment, relieve the oppressed, judge (deliver)
the fatherless, plead for the widow." (Is. 1:17)

As an arm of the local church, the Rescue Mission
reaches those the church, in most cases, cannot reach.
God has used this Mission in a mighty way, and I am very
grateful. For you see, without the concern of Brother Neal
Wilcox and the staff, Temple Baptist would be minus five
of its members.

What a real blessing and asset they are to our church family! For the most part, they are very faithful and take an active part in the activities of Temple Baptist Church. There have been times that our members from the Mission have helped with the grounds keeping, building maintenance, and music. Rev. Bill Fryar, the Mission manager, is also a member of Temple Baptist and serves as one of our deacons. Moreover, he was ordained into the Gospel ministry and commissioned into the Rescue Mission ministry by our church.

Some pastors and church members may have doubts as to whether or not mission men can function in the local church setting as well as add to its ministry in the community. May I remind you, dear reader, getting the men into local Bible-believing churches is one important step toward getting them back into society as fruitful believers. Quite frankly, here is one pastor who has no doubts regarding the effectiveness of the mission members. These dear men are precious to our local fellowship, and we love and appreciate them. They are growing in the Lord and are willing to help wherever and whenever possible. "Now we exhort you, brethren, warn them that are unruly, comfort the feebleminded, support the weak, be patient toward all *men.*" (1 Thes. 5:14)

> Abraham Lincoln said: "You cannot build character and courage by taking away man's initiative and independence. You cannot help men permanently by doing for them what they could and should do for themselves."

* * *

Dear Rev. Wilcox

I thought I would write you a few lines to let you know how much the Jackson family appreciates what you did for us. I pray that God will give you the strength to carry on the good work. I want to thank the other men who would go in and have prayer with my loved one. If there was no rescue mission, I don't know what men on the street would do. They should be proud of a man like you to take them in and give them a place to stay, food to eat, and the opportunity to hear the word of God preached every day. It means everything to know someone cares for others like you do. I pray God will bless you, and I thank you for everything.

The Jackson family

* * *

Rev. Wilcox and mission,

We, the Shelton family wish to take this opportunity to thank all of you who were so nice to us on our visit to Winston-Salem. While it was a visit of sorrow you all made it a lot easier and we thank you for it. We thank you all for what you did for William the past few years. May God continue to bless the work and all that's concerned with it and may you reach many souls for God's glory.

The Shelton family

(Mr. Bill Shelton was dedicated to the Mission for a number of years in food service.)

* * *

Dear Rev. Wilcox,

I am writing concerning the help you gave us. We had nothing left except each other, when our home was destroyed by fire January 23, 1985. We called the rescue mission and you gave us hope in God's word, as well as clothing and furniture, please express our gratitude to all of those concerned with the mission. It's such a comfort to know there are people we can turn to in time of need. God bless you all and thank you.

Gratefully yours,
R. and M. Moore and children

* * *

Dear Mr. Wilcox

I am sorry I didn't write you sooner. We have been very busy. We are doing pretty well now. After the funeral I had a rough two weeks. The Sunday after the funeral we started going back to church and my husband got saved. Since then I have been saved, even my sister's husband has gotten saved. I believe I will see daddy again. I'm just so thankful he found somebody like you. Because he was a great father before he started drinking. I'm so glad daddy finally had some happiness in his life. If anybody deserves it, he did. The reason I'm writing I would like to come and see you. I heard you have church services at the rescue mission, please let me know when you have them.

Praise God we love you,
T. M. Spellman

AFTERWORD

———————•———————

There has been no greater joy in my life than to "Serve the Lord with gladness...." (Ps. 100:2) Praise be to the Lord for choosing this most unlikely man to carry His message of love and hope to the helpless and hopeless people of the streets; for filling the heart of a fatherless young boy with compassion for the forgotten man.

Thank you for taking the time to walk with me through the memories of my life and experiences—experiences of joys and sorrows. Whether family, friends, or strangers, I hope and pray you have felt my heart—with all of its hurts and its happiness. While I was writing this book, Barbara once told a friend, "Sometimes I hear him laughing, and sometimes I hear him crying." Someone once said, "It takes sunshine as well as rain to make a rainbow." I believe the Lord has blessed me with far more sunshine than rain, and through it all, my Lord remains the same.

As the sun goes down on my life, I want you to know that if you do not know my Lord as your Savior, the Son can come up in your life if you will only acknowledge your need and ask Him to come into your heart. I have prayed for you. I pray every person who reads this book would receive the message God has for them within its pages. God is good and ready to forgive, and if you come by faith and trust in Him, you will be met with His sufficiency for all your needs, just as He has provided in my life.

I hope to meet you one day where the sun will never set and listen to the story of your journey through life by God's grace.

CPSIA information can be obtained at www.ICGtesting.com
Printed in the USA
LVOW06s0658150814

399172LV00001BA/1/P